St. Scholastica Library
Duluth, Minnesota 55811

Anglo-American Philosophy of Law

Anglo-American Philosophy of Law

An Introduction to Its Development and Outcome

Beryl Harold Levy

Transaction Publishers
New Brunswick (U.S.A.) and London (U.K.)

KD
640
.L48
1990

Copyright © 1991 by Transaction Publishers,
New Brunswick, New Jersey 08903

All rights reserved under International and Pan-American Copyright Conventions. No part of this book may be reproduced or transmitted in any form or by any means, electronic or mechanical, including photocopy, recording, or any information storage and retrieval system, without prior permission in writing from the publisher. All inquiries should be addressed to Transaction Publishers, Rutgers-The State University, New Brunswick, New Jersey 08903.

Library of Congress Catalog Number: 90-39537
ISBN: 0-88738-344-0
Printed in the United States of America

Library of Congress Cataloging-in-Publication Data

Levy, Beryl Harold, 1908–
    Anglo-American philosophy of law : an introduction to its development and outcome / Beryl Harold Levy.
      p. cm.
    Includes index.
    ISBN 0-88738-344-0
    1. Law—Great Britain—Philosophy. 2. Law—United States--Philosophy. 3. Natural law. 4. Legal positivism. I. Title.
KD640.L48   1990
340′.1—dc20   90-39537
                                            CIP

To
Thea and Phyllis
and
COLUMBIA

Contents

Preface — ix
Acknowledgments — xiii
Introduction — xv

Part I Varieties of Natural Law — 1

1. Varieties of Natural Law — 3

Part II The Utilitarian Revolt and Legal Positivism — 17

2. Jeremy Bentham (1748–1832): The Shift to Consequences — 21
3. John Austin (1790–1859): The Separation of Law and Morality — 29
4. John Stuart Mill (1806–1873): Liberty — 37

Part III The American Fruitions — 41

5. Thomas Jefferson (1743–1826): Equality — 43
6. Oliver Wendell Holmes, Jr. (1871–1947): The Pragmatic Turn — 49
7. Roscoe Pound (1870–1964): Sociological Jurisprudence — 77
8. John Dewey (1859–1953): The Activities of Law — 81
9. Karl N. Llewellyn (1893–1962): Legal Realism — 87
10. Benjamin N. Cardozo (1870–1938): The Judicial Process — 93

11. Lon Fuller (1902–1978): The Rise of Law — 101
12. H. L. A. Hart (1907–   ): The Validity of Law — 109

Part IV Summary Observations — 117

13. The Realist Outcome — 119

A Bibliographic Chat — 133

Index — 137

Preface

By the time we reach the twentieth century, we have accumulated such superabundant accounts of the past that no one can encompass even a small part of what is known about the Greeks or Romans or Anglo-Saxons or even our own American culture. Unavoidably we have to choose; our criterion of choice depends upon our purpose. If we want to prove something, for example, our selection will be made to support our argument. For a description of the criterion of selection in my own descriptive survey, I borrow the words of Crane Brinton:

> Still another principle of choice, in intellectual history at least, might be to take the figures which the general opinion of cultivated people today has marked out as classics, as the great thinkers and writers, and outline as clearly and succinctly as possible what they wrote.

He adds, "Now this is worth doing."

This has been done in histories of philosophy and histories of political theory. Many books and articles have presented professional and technical analyses of the thought of these great thinkers. Here I proffer distillations of their thought to bring out the bearing their thought has had on legal philosophy as it was accepted by educated persons in later societies. After a background account of natural law, I focus on the culminations in Anglo-American philosophy of law as I have observed and experienced them. Our country is only two hundred years old, and, since I was born in 1908, I have lived through most of its second century.

The autonomy of anyone's mind proceeds out of a given tradition. We all have to step into the stream, as the Chinese proverb has it. I have included a personal introduction to reveal the incidence of my own approach.

I have tried to write as simply and plainly as I could. I have aimed to explain philosophers to lawyers, lawyers to philosophers, and both to students and to the general reader. Thus I have avoided footnotes, legal and academic citations, and professional jargon. I have shunned legalese and academese and pedantries. Neil MacCormick, in expressing the hope that his book, *Legal Reasoning and Legal Theory,* will be of interest not only to nonexperts but also to lawyers and philosophers, speaks for all of us plowing this field:

> I have therefore tried to write in such a way that it will be comprehensible to nonphilosophical lawyers and to nonlawyer philosophers. Each group will find a great deal which is from its own point of view rather elementary and obvious, for which I apologize in advance. Conversely, I hope that neither group will find undue obscurities in the less familiar points of the text.

In addition I have made a special effort to reach the nonspecialist reader and student. To attain that goal, I have had to forego detailed analyses of points at issue among legal philosophers waging polemical wars.

I am, of course, only too well aware that there are plenty of alternative and fuller interpretations of these complex figures, and that others might have been included. I make no pretense to comprehensiveness or avoidance of secondary sources. My goal has been to stay within manageable proportions for a streamlined perspective which would help me to understand where we are and where we came from, and to share that understanding.

By ending with H. L. A. Hart, I forego discussion of younger, contemporary analysts among his followers, whose names are familiar to scholars in this field: inter alia, Dworkin, Feinberg, Greenawalt, MacCormick, Morris, Sartorius, Wasserstrom, Wollhelm, et al. Though I am working a side of the street different from theirs both in style and scope, I am indebted to their writings and personal discussion.

On the side of philosophy, I am happy to note the 1988 address of the current president of the American Philosophical Association (Eastern Division), Richard Bernstein. After the bitter split in philosophical circles in America in recent years, a split caused by the vogue of "analytic" philosophy and its rejection of any other way of "doing" philosophy, Bernstein welcomes the arrival of a spirit of pluralism and the renewal of pragmatism. This pluralism extends to the interplay of disciplines such as philosophy and law. He reminds us that what William James wrote in 1904 is again relevant at the present moment. There is a

> curious unrest in the philosophic atmosphere of the time, a loosening of old landmarks, a softening of oppositions, a mutual borrowing from one another . . . as if the one thing sure was the inadequacy of the extant school-solutions. The dissatisfaction with these seems due for the most part to a feeling that they are too abstract and academic.

The younger generation, he notes, would like to inject more life into its philosophy, even though it were at some cost of logical and formal purity. Pragmatism nurtures pluralism "that is based upon mutual respect, where we are willing to risk our own prejudgments, are open to listening and learning from others, and we respond to others with responsiveness and responsibility."

I regret that I have not yet mastered a non-gender style and I hope the reader will indulge "man" to embrace "woman."

Acknowledgments

Irving Louis Horowitz, president of Transaction Publishers, took hold of this book in its penultimate form and encouraged me to whip it into manageable shape. The manuscript benefited greatly from the collegial generosities of my friend, Abraham Edel. The trustees authorized a grant from the John Dewey Foundation to study Dewey's contributions to legal philosophy. From time to time, I have enjoyed the confidences of Walter Gellhorn, who extended an invitation to me to return to the Columbia Law School as a Visiting Scholar. Although my sympathies lie with these fellow pragmatists, I wish also to thank several "analytical" philosophers. Kent Greenawalt, a disciple of H. L. A. Hart, brought me up to date in his current seminar. Joel Feinberg invited me to his stimulating sessions at Rockefeller University. Richard Wasserstrom included me in the summer program of the Council of Philosophic Studies. I am not a historiographer, and the section on natural law rests heavily (though not entirely) on the scholarship and analyses of Richard Wollheim and Wolfgang Friedmann. The reference librarians at the Babylon Public Library, Andrew Hamm and Patricia La Ware, brought me needed material from near and far. The New York Public Library extended the privileges of the Writers' Room. My wife, Phyllis, and daughter, Thea, gave me the benefit of their critical judgment, editoral help, and moral support, without which this book could hardly have happened. My editor, Esther Luckett, has been exemplary in details of style and thought. Sheldon Finkelstein did a lawyer-like job on the proofs.

In expressing my indebtedness to all of them I am of course exculpating them from any complicity in the strategy of this book or its errors and shortcomings.

Introduction

Personal Introduction: How This Book Came to Be Put Together

When I was an undergraduate at Columbia University (1925–29), I found a climate of opinion which began to shape my mind in a way which my later studies as a Columbia graduate student and at the Columbia Law School deepened. I am relating that experience to explain how I came to put this book together. As I. F. Stone has said, "No book can be fully understood unless the writer discloses the motivation that led him to embark on his onerous task."

Mine could be taken as a parochial experience limited to the ferments at Columbia University, except that John Dewey's influence was at its height, not only there but throughout the country, because of his public activities and his many books on various phases of public events. At the same time, Dewey gave to academic philosophy the turn of thought which he at Columbia and William James at Harvard were developing as a distinctively American emphasis which James called "pragmatism." The temper of my own prelegal education enabled me to view our legal tradition more broadly in its philosophic implications.

Unlike many of my classmates at the college, I did not settle for the "gentleman's C" which was the vogue in those halcyon days of jazz-age prosperity, with its wild stock market before the crash in 1929, the year we graduated. The eminent lawyer, William Nelson Cromwell has related that it was the practice of his firm, Sullivan and Cromwell, to engage Ivy League college graduates with a "C" average prior to the crash, but thereafter his firm insisted on a high degree of scholarly attainment to meet the challenges of the post-Depression era. I plunged into the rich experience of Columbia University with enthusiasm.

Columbia College from that time to this day has had a core curriculum which all undergraduates were required to take as they also pursued their electives. It was called "Contemporary Civilization." It met five days a week at 9 A.M. in a small class. My instructor was James Gutmann, a young member of the Philosophy Department participating in the program.

I guess Gutmann could not help giving a philosophic orientation to the course, which was really about Western civilization, culminating in our own times—its politics, art, religion, science, and economics. I have ever since approached every subject from the vantage point of the full life we lead contemporaneously in its historical evolvements. We thought of Western civilization as the defender of those democratic freedoms for which World War I had been fought.

I cannot pinpoint at just what point I fell in love with philosophy, but I'm sure I was influenced also by a remarkable teacher, Irwin Edman, whose course, "Introduction to Philosophy," enthralled many of us. Edman and Gutmann and the other young instructors, Herbert Schneider, Richard McKeon and Horace Friess, welcomed me heartily into the department as I chose philosophy for my major. We thought of philosophy as an educational enterprise which should reach everyone, not ivory-towered but fraught with practical consequences.

We were required to read a book called *Reflective Thinking* by the "Columbia Associates." This book expounded the Deweyan spirit permeating the college. I did not then realize the extent to which it reflected pragmatism as the currently vital movement in American philosophy. I did not then realize the drastic reorientation given to the philosophical tradition by a small group of thinkers in Cambridge, Massachusetts, including William James, Charles Peirce, and the young Oliver Wendell Holmes, Jr., who (like myself, though I did not know it at the time) could not make up his mind whether to teach philosophy or go into law. (Here the resemblance between myself and the legendary Holmes ends.)

Another able intellectual lawyer, Greene, was also in this "Metaphysical Club," ironically so-called, and he was the greatest influence on Holmes. Peirce had initiated pragmatism as a method of making our ideas clear by relating them to their practical consequences, after the manner of experimental science. It was considered a method of analyzing ideas and had nothing to do, as James emphasized, with grand concepts and ultimate answers. Besides the influence upon them of the fruitfulness of the scientific way of thinking, we can make a case for the strong influence of the lawyers' way of thinking as well.

When we speak of practical consequences, we do not mean practical in the bread-and-butter sense; we mean all possible consequences. The cardinal point is that we test all ideas by their consequences and not by their conformity to some antecedent principle.

To engage in the exercise of human intelligence called "reflective thinking" meant to turn one's back on absolutes and certainties, on dogmas and the supposed traditional truths of reason. It meant recognizing that, as Isaiah Berlin says, John Locke's empiricism is the central tradition in English, and, especially, American philosophy, appealing to everyone's observation and experience.

As I went on with my philosophy studies, I found that the course in formal logic was being dropped from the curriculum and that the Announcement of Courses of Instruction included philosophy in the same announcement as psychology and anthropology. I noticed a disposition in the Philosophy Department to edge philosophy toward the social sciences. In his book *Reconstruction in Philosophy,* in a later edition changed to *Reconstruction of Philosophy,* Dewey declared that philosophy is most significant when it deals with the problems of men and not the problems of philosophers. Philosophers should develop philosophy as a method for coping with the problems of men and solving them, not intellectually, but through intelligently helping to actually alter the unsatisfactory situations which caused the problem to arise. His model for effective thinking was not Rodin's statue of the seated Thinker, elbow on knee, head on fist; Dewey's example of effective thinking was that of an engineer who designs blueprints for a bridge and continues his directives until the bridge is built and we can get across the river. The problematic situation was actually and practically resolved by the sought-for change, which would lick the problem in our experience and not only in our minds. No wonder for that generation, Roscoe Pound's characterization of the law as "social engineering" has a copacetic ring.

"Radical empiricism" would not overlook any relevant experience and would include all relevant experiences. Empirical philosophy does not come across by its logical structure but by its relation to the times—the people and issues of the times. There are no eternal truths, and change is a fact of life. Philosophy, like law, addresses itself to particular situations or contexts. On a cultural level it would try to clarify art or science or law or religion or education as human interests and problems crying for continuous clarification and solution.

In the "Contemporary Civilization" course, we leaned heavily on John Randall's book *The Making of the Modern Mind,* a book which made a great impression on me, especially as I followed it up by Randall's course in the "History of Philosophy." I saw how empirical philosophers handled philosophic materials historically by recounting trends and summarizing leading figures. Schneider was doing the same for his book *A History of American Philosophy.* True to the conviction that philosophy is not an isolated intellectuality but an organic part of a whole culture, Schneider advised his readers to supplement his book by reading Dorfman's history of American economics and Schlesinger's political history. I recall Schneider poking fun at the glass flowers in the Harvard museum. How can you know anything about flowers if you don't see them growing in their habitat?

I worked with Edman in philosophy of art and with Friess and Schneider in philosophy of religion and I pursued social philosophy throughout. In my special concentrations at the college I studied Plato with Edman, Aristotle and Spinoza with McKeon, Hume with Storck. I also studied the classics of the Western world in a seminar with a handful of students and two instructors, Mark Van Doren and Mortimer Adler. Adler was then in the Psychology Department, as he did not go along with the Deweyan Philosophy Department. Today both the contemporary civilization and the humanities classics courses have been enlarged to include oriental civilization.

In my account thus far, I trust I have begun to prepare the reader for the kind of exposition he or she can expect in this book: empirically describing the legal philosophies in their historical trends.

Upon graduating in 1929, I was offered a fellowship in the Philosophy Department to participate in the graduate seminar on American philosophy and religion. After three years of graduate study (Ph.D. 1933), with a dissertation under Herbert Schneider, I was still faced with the continuing Depression, and I entered the Columbia School of Law at the same time F. D. R. was launching the New Deal. I did not know if I would practice law, but I was intrigued by law as an impressive example of the effort to solve practical social problems though a cumulative intellectual discipline of its own. During the summers I had been teaching philosophy at City College, where Morris Raphael Cohen, a friend of Holmes and Felix Frankfurter, was the first philosophy professor to give a course in the philosophy of law.

At the law school I again encountered Dewey's influence, since he had been giving, at the law school, a seminar on philosophy of law, and I also encountered Mortimer Adler's influence as he worked with Professor Michael on the logic of evidence. Karl Llewellyn was then vigorously launching the Legal Realist movement in the spirit of Dewey, whom he greatly admired. Dewey was a vivid influence on Llewellyn, who liked nothing more than to be likened to Dewey. I was already so formed by the empiricism of my seven years exposure that I naturally gravitated to Llewellyn, a rich and broad and talented personality, a man of culture and literary as well as legal ability, and ablaze with his crusade to rescue the law from its old formalistic and conceptualistic format. He was doing for law what Dewey had done for philosophy. I entered heartily into his crusade.

I could not have imagined that the two distinguished senior professors at the law school today, Herbert Wechsler and Walter Gellhorn, would follow respectively the momentum of Michael and Adler and the momentum of Llewellyn and his fellow-Realist, Herman Oliphant.

To help support myself at law school I acted as research assistant to Professor Robert Lee Hale, whose province was law and economics and who seemed to me, by bringing his economic training to bear, also to be realistically broadening the law and repudiating a narrow self-sufficiency. Hale's book, *Freedom through Law*, combined his knowledge of institutional economics with his mastery of Constitutional law, and he demonstrated the scope of our liberty as protected by the Fourteenth Amendment: "No state shall deprive a person of life, liberty or property except by due process of Law." Hale was at pains to show how our liberty, in a realistic economic sense, is often curbed not only by a state statute in violation of the Fourteenth Amendment, but also by non-state "unofficial governments," as, for example, by a political party when only one party dominates the state, or by a labor union when it discriminates in a closed shop.

The other professor I worked for was Elliot Cheatham, who was inaugurating a new course called "The Legal Profession" to replace a legal ethics course with discussion of actual situations confronted by lawyers forced to make moral decisions bearing on their professional responsibility.

Professor M. R. Cohen's son, Felix, had a Ph.D. from Harvard before entering the Columbia Law School, and, like myself, enlisted heartily in Llewellyn's new movement. Like myself, he later worked at the law but also wrote and taught. We lost a great legal philosopher when he died at a lamentably early age while on the faculty of the Yale Law School. The compendium he started with his father and finished alone after his father's death, *Readings in Jurisprudence and Legal Philosophy* (1951), is a neglected treasure trove. A few rubrics will convey its scope: Legal Institutions, (such as torts, contracts, property), Theory of Law (in relation to the judicial process and legislation), Law and Philosophy (logic, ethics, metaphysics), and Law and Social Science (history, economics, anthropology, politics). When Felix Cohen died at the height of his powers as a lecturer both at Yale Law School and at City College (having succeeded to his father's legal philosophy course), I was asked to take over that course for a few years. I tried to use the Cohen and Cohen compendium but I found it too difficult for undergraduates. I believe it was then I first knew I would like to write a book like this one.

Because law school training drew us all into that phase of "legal realism" having to do with the appellate judicial process, I was much attracted to Cardozo's book *The Nature of the Judicial Process* and in Llewellyn's seminar I started my book, *Cardozo and Frontiers of Legal Thinking*.

Professor Allison Dunham, then teaching at Columbia, invited me on behalf of the law faculty to develop the course in the

Columbia School of General Studies on "Law and Society," which included jurisprudence. Thus began my lifelong interest in presenting legal matters to nonlawyers in a nontechnical and humanistic fashion. Later I continued such courses for adults at the New School, while continuing to practice law at Kaye, Scholer, Fierman, Hays (and now Handler), and later in my own office. Professor Harold J. Berman deserves great credit for his continuous interest in such a program, and I was happy to be invited later to his Harvard symposium on "Law in the Liberal Arts Curriculum" along with Archibald McLeish (whom I urged in vain to write a poem about lawyers), McGeorge Bundy, Paul Herzog, and Daniel Boorstin, whose book on Blackstone, *The Mysterious Science of the Law,* I much admired. From Harvard came Paul Freund and Lon Fuller, from Yale Eugene Rostow, and from Columbia, along with myself, Harry Jones.

When I decided to put to use my studies of the judicial process, I took a post as Federal Administrative Law Judge, having been especially active in adminstrative law, which appealed to me as relating the law directly to political economy. I had learned administrative law, a new branch of legal study, from Professor Walter Gellhorn, who has made many contributions of a nonphilosophic, nonconceptualistic nature, such as, notably, his study of the Ombudsman in European countries for possible adoption here to handle citizen complaints against abuses by administrative agencies. I have enjoyed the benefit of Professor Gellhorn's advice and encouragement for many years. I noted with interest that he felt close to Charles Frankel, a professor of philosophy at Columbia who was also a student of Gutmann, Randall, and Edman and who moved into the Law School faculty in later years.

Since an empiricist addresses himself to the vital issues of his day, my next book was on the Constitution, written at the time of the excitement of the Roosevelt court-packing threat. Attorney General Robert H. Jackson wrote the introduction.

When I left active law practice to become an administrative judge, I reviewed my experience and observations at the bar in characteristic empirical fashion in a book called *Corporation Lawyer,* in which I traced the movement in the United States from lawyers as mainly courtroom lawyers to today's new type of lawyer, the office lawyer who deals in corporate strategems.

Many jurisprudents in recent years have concentrated on the analysis of language and its terms and concepts, in the manner of the English "analytic" philosophers. I myself have not followed this current because my empirical penchant is away from analyses which are simply logico-linguistic and which separate law and philosophy from their functional role in human culture. But I have benefited from the meticulous analyses of American analytical legal philosophers whose writings I know and whom I have heard lecture or known personally, including Feinberg, Morris, Wohlheim, and Wasserstrom, whom I met in Irvine, California, at a seminar in legal philosophy of the Council of Philosophic Studies. Dworkin, who teaches both at Oxford and New York University, has been prolific. The conferences and publications of the American Society of Legal and Political Philosophy have been rewarding, as has been my participation in Amintaphil, the American branch of the International Association for Legal and Social Philosophy. At the world congress in Brussels, Pincoffs, Jenkins, and myself were on a panel on "Justification of a Judicial Decision," and Pincoffs remarked on the remarkable resemblance of our analyses, despite our diverse backgrounds. Jenkins and I started a correspondence, which continued for many years, over his book which appeared, in its refreshing independence, with the title *Social Order and the Limits of Law*.

Upon retiring as an Administrative Judge, I turned to teaching at Hofstra University. I offered courses in what the dean liked to call "cultural jurisprudence." I retired from that post as Professor Emeritus of Philosophy and Social Science. I then gave similar courses at the New School for Social Research. After a further mandatory retirement, I decided to put this primer together. I had considerable doubts about so simplified an account, but these were overcome by the enthusiastic encouragement of my friend, Irving Louis Horowitz, who is the Distinguished Professor of Sociology at Rutgers and the president of Transaction Publishers, my publisher.

I am of two minds about this personal introduction because scholarly conventions favor a more austere pose and look askance at mists of egoism. But I thought it would also serve a purpose as an exhibit of one person's reminiscences of his encounters with legal philosophy as it climaxed in Legal Realism. There are not many of us left, and as an octogenarian I hope I am immune from any suspicion of some ulterior motive of aggrandizement.

One instance of the inspiration of Legal Realism is the emphasis on an innovative judicial technique known as "Prospective overruling," which I have explored elsewhere in a law review article. Prospective overruling is an example of the willingness of American judges to apply legal philosophy to the judicial process, as in Justice Cardozo's philosophic defense of the technique in the *Sunburst* case and the references in the subsequent *Linkletter* case to Blackstone, Austin, Gray, and Holmes.

Aims of this Book

In this book I combine two aims. I am trying to convey a survey of legal theory from its earliest roots in natural law, through its English development in legal positivism, to its fruitions in the Legal Realist movement in the United States. At the same time, I seek to make vivid the influence of the distinctive American philosophy of pragmatism as it is reflected in the movement of Legal Realism and the realist outcome.

I have already recited the education and experience which involved me in philosophic pragmatism and legal realism and the writing of this book.

Legal theory has always been inspired by forces outside the law in philosophy or politics. In America in the first half of the twentieth century, the influence came from the philosophy of pragmatism, the most vital movement on the American scene, spearheaded by William James at Harvard and John Dewey at Columbia. Some critics have noted an alliance between the surge of the New Deal and the movement of Legal Realism, but I am inclined to think their appearance at roughly the same time was a coincidence and that the seeds of Legal Realism antedated the New Deal.

By the twentieth century, the legal profession had become so well organized in America and law schools had become so proficient that legal theory arose in a highly professional environment from among lawyers and the law professoriate.

After sketching the background of varieties of natural law in the ancient, medieval, and modern worlds, I presented the leading figures and trends in England and then in America, which "received" the common law of England and its precedent system.

In England Hobbes and Locke, the fountainheads of English political and legal thought, were still involved with natural law in the seventeenth century, as they struggled to give a rationale for government after the divine right of kings had been discredited. Hooker is not known as well as Hobbes and Locke, but I regard him as an important link for legal philosophy in the compromise of king and Parliament and as the author of the first real treatise in England on law proper.

In the eighteenth century, Bentham led the Utilitarian revolt against the "natural law" which had dominated legal theory for eighteen centuries. His colleague, John Austin, formulated the definitive articulation of the alternative legal theory known as "legal positivism," which took over in England and America.

In America Holmes embraced Austin and, in his pivotal article "The Path of the Law," he gave legal positivism his own inimitable expression, combining it with his pragmatic turn of mind. I have carefully dissected Holmes's essay as it contains his main thought with all its pregnancies. Holmes is the towering figure in American legal thought, and I invite close attention to his opulent essay.

Holmes and John Dewey admired each other, and Dewey, though not primarily a legal philosopher, was the main influence on Karl Llewellyn, who launched the movement known as Legal Realism, which changed the temper of American law.

I do not want to play with words, but both the word *realism* and the word *pragmatism* are what Theodore Roosevelt called "weasel words," like the related words *empirical* and *positivist*. I am not interested in "isms" (which encrust thought) or labels (which are often libels), but these terms need to be clarified for nonphilosophers. James did refer to pragmatic method as a thoroughgoing "empiricism" and Llewellyn might just as well have spoken of the movement of "legal realism" as "legal empiricism" or "legal pragmatism." He was simply coordinating and expressing the attitude which had become evident in the advanced (not to say avant-garde) thinking of law professors in the 1920s. He liked nothing more than to be likened to John Dewey. He chose the term *realism* wisely, I think, to avoid complicating its reception by reference to the lingo of philosophers. Like every empirical thinker since Locke, he was interested in observables and in experiences and their consequences, not in a priori or antecedent principles, or a priori truths of reason. A thesaurus offers, as synonyms for *empirical,* "experiential, pragmatic, provisional, practical." There is also the component of experimental. I hesitate to involve the reader in the finesses of this term *positivism,* but as "logical positivism" or "logical empiricism" it invaded English philosophy in this century via the Vienna Circle, where A. J. Ayer brought it to England as a method akin to pragmatic method. On its "logical" side, it led to a group of English "analytical" philosophers who influenced and gave rise to analytical legal philosophers. With American pragmatism, the emphasis was rather on the social involvements and the interrelations of science and ethics, resulting in a mood of confident encouragement of social science. We find it, in philosophy, in Dewey and, in law, in Llewellyn.

Roscoe Pound, a Harvard colleague of James, agreed with James that, on the level of immediate or practical experience, we are face-to-face with human wants. Pound thinks the law should satisfy human wants as much as feasible. He calls it "social engineering," and the implication is that human wants should be weighed and brought into some kind of balance through social arrangements brought about by law. I am not sure the term is a happy one, because the law is the law and not engineering. But the metaphor is an apt one, because the model of the engineer used to be described by Dewey, when I took his course in "Experimental Logic", as exemplary of pragmatic thinking. The engineer not only makes blueprints, but supervises the actual construction of the bridge until we can cross it and get to the other side.

Following from Pound's "sociological jurisprudence," Karl Llewellyn and Jerome Frank consolidated various extant trends among legal thinkers and launched the movement of Legal Realism, which is the pragmatic outcome of Anglo-American philosophy. Oliver Wendell Holmes Jr. is its godfather. The reader is urged to study Holmes closely. In an edition of his *Collected Legal Papers* which appeared in 1920, he remarked with accuracy and pride:

> A later generation has carried on the work that I began nearly half a century ago, and it is a great pleasure to an old warrior who cannot expect to bear arms much longer, that the brilliant young soldiers still give him a place in their councils of war.

The brilliant young soldiers were the very Legal Realists at the climax of this book.

A Road Map to the Book

In part 1, I have treated natural law in all its various incarnations, culminating in the eighteenth century with its denouement in our own Declaration of Independence, based on "nature and nature's God" and the "higher" law background of our Constitution and Bill of Rights. I do not dwell on the emergence of human rights as a cardinal emphasis in the contemporary world only because it would take us beyond the bounds of our subject, Anglo-American theory of law, which I am doing my best to keep manageable.

The theme announced in my title, "Anglo-American Philosophy of Law," is presented *in extenso* in part 2, where I devote chapters to the English development in the Utilitarian philosophers Jeremy Bentham, John Austin, and John Stuart Mill; I set their views forth in the measured distillation, as sympathetically as I could, often in their own words and spirit.

In part 3, we move to America. After an initial chapter on Thomas Jefferson, I turn to Oliver Wendell Holmes, Jr., who, in the late nineteenth and early twentieth century, picked up legal positivism and gave it the momentum of his own unequalled scholarship, legal experience, and authoritative voice. At the same time, Holmes, who was a cofounder initially, together with Peirce, James, and Greene, of the distinctive American philosophy of pragmatism, gave to legal positivism a pragmatic turn. He thought there had been no jurisprudence worth the name prior to Austin, and he reinforced Austin's decisive separation of law from morals. His pragmatic turn came in his insistence that general principles or rules of law do not decide concrete cases; that in any given judicial decision there are competing values to be resolved, though they are usually unavowed because of the formal conventions of the format of judicial opinions; and that to a lawyer, dealing with the client's interests and the courts, the law is nothing more pretentious than the prediction of what a court is likely to decide in the given situation. In the chapter on Holmes I purposely do not set forth his views fully or in detail, because I have decided that I must urge the reader to read carefully for himself Holmes's great essay "The Path of the Law"; instead, to that end, I have very carefully dissected the essay, and provided subheadings to facilitate its profound and gravid re-directions.

Holmes is the godfather of the law movement known as Legal Realism; Legal Realism appeared among enlightened legal thinkers in the 1920s and 1930s, and I devote chapters 8 through 10 to four of these thinkers. Legal Realism was correlated and expounded with great force by Karl Llewellyn at the Columbia Law School, where I encountered it as his student. This movement, christened "Legal Realism," had much in common with Dean Roscoe Pound's "Sociological Jurisprudence" and received an auspicious fruitage in Judge Benjamin N. Cardozo's candid and realistic confession of how he goes about deciding cases. I have included John Dewey here, less because of his standing as a jurisprudent, than because of his great influence on his colleague at Columbia, Llewellyn, and because of the views he shared with Justice Holmes, whom he greatly admired.

I have treated Legal Realism as the climax of my account and as the "realistic outcome" to which my title alludes. But in chapters 11 and 12 I have also included the later views of Lon Fuller and H. L. A. Hart, who strike out in other directions. None of the blind men of the Indian legend grasped the whole elephant, and a consistent pragmatist would want to recontextualize as new developments emerge.

In part 4 I present a brief recapitulation in which my summary observations underscore the realist human outcome which has been a principle emphasis in my account.

Well, here is your baedeker. Now to the thinkers themselves! I have also tried to set up signposts as we go along; rather too much clarity of emphasis than too much perpetuated confusion.

I

VARIETIES OF NATURAL LAW

1

Varieties of Natural Law

The term "natural law" designates a theory which holds that law necessarily has a moral basis and that its criteria are grounded in something more than ordinary experience—in "nature." Natural law accepts as viable the quest for an absolute ideal of justice.

When we speak of natural law—or the laws of nature—the term "law" is deemed to convey a "higher law" than the existent laws, an "unwritten law" couched in very general terms and deemed to be everywhere the same, unchangeable, and enduring.

The term "nature" in laws of nature has been diversely interpreted in the variety of natural law theories which have emerged through the centuries.

Doctrinal Analysis

The first account of natural law is encountered in the works of Zeno (ca. 335–ca.263 B.C.), a Greek philosopher who founded the philosophy of Stoicism, a universal philosophy for a time of empire.

Zeno adverted to the concept of "nature," in the sense that the term was used by the early Greek "natural philosophers," who sought to ascertain the substance of the universe. Was it the elements of water, fire, earth, and air, as Empedocles taught, or atoms and the void, as Democritus taught? Instead of elements or atoms, Zeno taught that the universe consists of one substance which he called "nature."

According to Zeno, nature pervades the universe. Nature also rules the universe. This view of nature as ruling differs from that of the Hebrews, who conceived of the universe as ruled by their God, Yahweh.

These early philosophers did not expound their views critically, and I must ask the reader's patience as I summarize Zeno's view elliptically. Zeno identified "nature" with "reason." He used the terms interchangeably. To speak of the law of nature or the law of reason is identical. Thus the universe may also be said to be ruled by reason.

Nature being the same as reason and man being a part of nature, reason dwells in man—in each man everywhere.

Besides identifying nature with reason, Zeno identified nature and reason with God. Reason is divine reason which rules and binds men everywhere. Men are obliged to follow this universal natural law.

Man can avoid this obligation and can choose to obey or disobey this natural law, but, because he is rational, man acts in accordance with his reason insofar as he obeys natural law.

Cicero (106–43 B.C.), the eminent Roman lawyer, went to Greece for his education and became a Stoic. He followed Zeno in identifying nature and reason. He accepted nature or reason as ruling the universe. In his work, *De Re Publica,* Cicero also identified law as reason coextensive with nature. Cicero is the definitive classical locus for natural law, and I quote his famous summary:

> There is in in fact a true law—namely, right reason—which is in accordance with nature, applies to all men, and is unchangeable and eternal. By its commands this law summons men to the performance of their duties; by its prohibitions it restrains them from doing wrong. Its commands and prohibitions always influence good men, but are without effect on the bad. To invalidate the law by human legislation is never morally right, nor is it permissable ever to restrict its operations, and to annul it wholly is impossible. Neither the Senate nor the people absolve us from our obligation to obey the law. . . . It will not lay down one rule at Rome and another at Athens, nor will it be one rule today and another tomorrow. But there will be one law, eternal and unchangeable, binding at all times upon all peoples; and there will be, as it were, one common master and ruler of men, namely God, who is the author of this law, its interpreter and its sponsor. The man who will not obey it will abandon his better self and, in denying the true nature of a man, will thereby suffer the severest of penalties, though he has escaped all the other consequences which men call punishment.

As Cicero undertakes to give examples of natural law, he takes recourse to such generalities as "one should not harm another" or "if attacked one may defend oneself." He ridicules the idea that the law of a particular nation can be regarded as just law simply because it is the law in that nation. To Cicero it appears manifestly unjust, for example, for a tyrant to put to death anyone he wants to without a trial. If a state were to enact a law permitting theft, Cicero says, it would no more deserve to be called law than the rules passed by a band of robbers.

This conception of natural law as (1) *emanating from nature* and (2) *telling us what to do* was severely criticized by John Stuart Mill (1806–1873). Mill pointed out that it confused two separate things: (1) a law in the sense of a description of nature and (2) a law in the sense of a standard to which our conduct ought to conform. Natural law runs together what we now call the scientific laws of nature with moral precepts which ideally men ought to obey.

One way to escape this confusion would be to assume that both kinds of law come from a divine will which is supernatural. We avoid this confusion, but at the cost of other complexities.

Another difficulty which the Stoic maxim of "follow nature" is that nature is so heterogeneous. What aspects of nature are we to follow as a guide to our moral behavior and an index to law? If we really try to follow nature, are we to emulate the organized busyness of bees or the supine conformities of sheep?

Aristotle addresses this difficulty by suggesting that each aspect of nature fulfills its own end through its distinctive actions. (The Greek word for 'end' is *telos* and Aristotle's concept of nature is known as *teleological*.) As a matter of ordinary common sense, no one supposes that it is really true that all the phenomena of nature are divided into distinctive kinds—that each kind has its own nature with its own end and that, in some sense, human excellence is linked up with the realization of a unique human end. Aristotle's teleological conception of nature has enjoyed remarkable persistence, though philosophers of science proclaim an end to teleology.

Thomas Aquinas is accountable for the continuity of teleology in the Christian tradition through his achievement in fusing Aristotle with the pervasive thought of the medieval era. His compromise has become dominant in the Roman Catholic church. I am indebted to Wolheim for this doctrinal analysis, and, since he told me he had studied the original sources, I ask leave to quote him at this point.

> It was the achievement of St. Thomas Aquinas that he managed, within a certain framework of thought, to solve what might be called the "selectivity" problem of natural law theory by grafting on to the Stoic principle of "follow nature" the Aristotelian concept of nature as a teleological system. The general principles of the law of nature are, St. Thomas argued, known equally to all through their use of reason, though with the derivative principles, which are exercises in practical not speculative reason, the same consensus cannot be expected.

After the Protestant Reformation, Aristotle's teleogical metaphysics was largely repudiated. For example, Grotius, a Dutch scholar, who laid the foundations of international law, based it on a nonmetaphysical version of natural law theory. To put it with extreme economy, he held that man's nature is identified with reason and that natural law is whatever is acceptable to human reason. Natural law is what human reason discovers, and natural law is discovered by human reason. We are, however, still left with the difficulty of knowing what "reason" is, a difficulty later tackled by the British empirical philosophers.

Teleological natural law theory was still further weakened with the proposal of still another sense for the term *nature* by the sevententh-century English philosophers, Thomas Hobbes and John Locke. They associated natural law with the concept "state of nature." They contrasted a governed state with a state of nature, that is, a state without government. The concept "state of nature" was identified with the concept "natural law."

We can return to the Roman Empire for still another sense in which the standards of justice are deemed to be grounded in nature but without any metaphysical involvements. In this version, nature is identified with the common element in the variety of legal codes in the various nations conquered by the Roman Empire. The Roman legal system included this body of law, which the Romans used whenever one of the litigants was not a Roman citizen. It was known as the *ius gentium*. The laws of each people were known as the *ius civile*. The Roman jurist Gaius (A.D. 160) contrasted *ius civile* with a law practiced by all mankind and dictated to all men by natural reason. For such natural law Gaius took for his model the *ius gentium*.

This highly empirical account of natural law—based on the observed experience of the various legal systems of the diverse peoples in the Roman Empire—has great appeal for me as one who thinks of himself as an empirical philosopher. But in those days, empirical philosophy—a philosophy based on observed experience rather than a priori reason—had not yet emerged as a standard way of philosophizing, and so such a theory could not for long stand by itself on its own empirical feet. A century after Gaius, the Roman jurist Ulpian again surrounded natural law with intricate terminological distinctions.

There is an important feature of natural law doctrine which looms large in public debates today both in England and America: the status imputed to any extant law which does not comply with natural law standards of justice. Even though such extant laws satisfy all the generally acknowledged criteria of legal validity, natural law theorists insist that they are not laws at all. Conformity to natural law is required not only for a just law, but for law itself. (Doubtless, we have here a partial explanation for the agitations about abortion.)

The theory of natural law was at last frontally challenged by John Austin (1790–1859): "the existence of law is one thing; its merit or demerit another thing"; there is no *necessary* connection between them. Through Austin, the alternative theory of "legal positivism" forcibly entered modern thought.

The conflict between natural law and legal positivism is not merely a quarrel about a definition. To have a theory which excludes a duly enacted law as unjust because it conflicts with the generalities of a presupposed natural law has important practical consequences. It is a wholesale condemnation which avoids the intellectual effort of making a choice in some specific situation or of having to choose between an allegedly unjust law and no law at all. When considering what should be enforced by law, natural law theorists start with their own moral basis—what men ought to do according to their morality. We are left with the vital question which confronts us today: Is it the function of law to *enforce* any morality—any morality whatsoever?

Let us itemize and illustrate the main constituents of natural law doctrine:

1. Natural law is an ideal to which extant "positive" law should stretch and conform.
2. Natural law *eventuates* in the indefeasible rights of the individual person.
3. Natural law is a "higher" law which can invalidate a positive law.
4. Natural law encompasses all men everywhere in the vision of a universal order.

The first point is reflected in Cardozo's denotation of justice as an "aspiration."

The second point is crystallized, as we shall see, in Locke's seventeenth-century theory, which becomes a revolutionary slogan in the eighteenth-century, and emerges on the world scene prominently in the twentieth-century as human rights.

The third point is found in post-Nazi courts of Germany nullifying Hitler's laws.

The fourth point undergirds the Universal Declaration of Human Rights of the United Nations.

English and American Developments

We turn now to the natural law component in the fountainheads of the modern English development of legal philosophy, Hobbes and Locke.

Before discussing the more familiar theories of Hobbes and Locke, let us examine the adroit and lesser-known earlier sixteenth-century compromise of Richard Hooker (1553–1600), an Anglican clergyman who duly recognized natural law in his *Law of Ecclesiastical Polity,* the first treatise in the English tradition directly geared to legal theory. Though his discussion revolves around church government, his philosophy can be taken to embrace general government. He was very influential in England. He built a bridge between natural law as interpreted by the Vatican and the authority of King Henry VIII, who had broken with the pope and established himself as the head of the Church of England. As he was an Anglican clergyman in the Church of England, Hooker acknowledged the king's claim to be head of the church. As a clergyman he was steeped in Aquinas's exposition of natural law.

He conceived of our ordinary positive law as part of the larger framework of natural law. But he could not accept the pope as the authoritative interpreter. He had to replace papal authority with a secular authority. The secular authority was no longer solely the king: Parliament was already asserting itself as the voice of the citizenry. Since the king was also the head of the Anglican church, the king-in-Parliament could replace the pope as interpreter of natural law.

Hooker spoke of natural law as the "law of reason": as that law which human nature knows itself "in reason universally bound unto." Human nature knows the "law of reason" and feels obliged to follow it by the light of "natural understanding." He also called it the "constitution."

(In our own day Robert Hutchins, a subscriber to a secular natural law doctrine, has also observed that natural law derives from human nature, but he adds that we still do not know all that much about human nature despite our increased knowledge.)

Hooker concludes that we are obliged to obey the law because it rests on reason, or because of its constitutional basis (for which the consent of the governed is essential). "The lawful power of making laws to command whole political societies belongs properly onto the same entire societies."

When the constitution is spoken of as resting on reason, we are leaning back on natural law. When we speak of the constitution as resting on the people's consent, we are marching forward into the future. We are obliged to obey the law because it is legitimized by the consent of the people.

Thomas Hobbes (1588–1679) set the tone for modern political and legal theory, doing so with the conceptual coinage circulating in his day. The three terms both he and Locke used are "natural law," "social contract," and "state of nature," the concepts I have previously mentioned as depicting a supposed condition of society before the advent of government.

Hobbes views men in their "state of nature" as selfish egoists at war with one another as they vie to allay their mutually aggressive insecurity. Man is able to escape this "state of nature" because man's natural reason drives him to self-preservation through the erection of an all-powerful ruler. Everyone accepts and obeys this ruler as preferable to the terrible insecurity of a state of nature marked by everyone's fear of sudden death. Each one gives up his individual power to the all-powerful sovereign who prevents men from mutually destroying one another. This is Hobbes's version of the social contract. The sovereign rules neither by divine right nor by natural law. The government is simply the useful creation of individuals, subscribed to in order to avoid the excesses of the state of nature.

For Hobbes, man is naturally at liberty, and law exists only for essential restraints. Hobbes sets up the conspicuous features of modern, middle-class, "capitalistic" man: individualistic, self-interested, competitive, respectful of power. What a contrast to the feudal manor and orthodox religion of medieval times or the organic community of the little Greek *polls,* where Plato viewed justice as the harmony in the individual's psyche, corresponding to the harmony of the structure of the state. The Canadian political philosopher MacPherson calls Hobbes's theory "possessive individualism."

Hobbes is a fountainhead because many streams flow from his masterwork, *Leviathan,* and his writings on law. As we shall see, he is confluent with Locke in taking the individual as the basic unit of society and with Bentham and Austin as a forerunner of their principles of utility and coercion.

Hobbes couldn't care less about natural law as some supreme perfection of law. Law to him is simply positive law: law laid down by the "sovereign." Plain and simple! No metaphysics, no chatter about nature. Man himself chooses the premises from which he reasons, and a natural law theory is nothing but precepts derived from the premises chosen. Law is simply what man constructs as law. Positive law is whatever the sovereign commands. The only law Hobbes is concerned about is the law of England. The rules of law are our own invention. We can make them as we please. If we make any jurisprudential statements about law in general, we must base them upon such positive laws.

(In our own generation, A. J. Ayer, the English *logical* positivist, [who claims to be in unison with the pragmatic method] finally condemned all the speculations of traditional philosophy as a worthless pursuit. The proposition of natural law that law is right by nature and not by human convention Ayer wrote off as a "pseudo-proposition" because we do not have any way of verifying its truth or falsity. It is not that it is false; it is just meaningless.)

Unlike Hobbes, John Locke lived through the peaceful Glorious Revolution of 1688 which established Parliament. Locke (1632–1704) spoke for the rising middle class, which had come into a prominence which has lasted to our own time.

Locke was able to weave together many different ideas to express the emancipation of the individual after the peaceful revolution of 1688. Locke was a physician and made the greatest contribution to law of any nonlawyer. His book had enormous influence despite its absence of logical rigor.

While taking over the concept of natural law as superior to positive law, Locke also exalted the individual by introducing inalienable natural "rights" including, prominently, the right to private property along with life and liberty. It was Locke who definitively converted natural law to natural rights.

Locke's social contract did not, like Hobbes's, transfer all of the individual's natural powers to the authority of the government. Locke used the notion of social contract to exhibit an agreement between the people, who by a majority set up a government to rule them, and the government, which in turn reciprocally promised to hold power in trust to preserve each individual's rights. Locke retained for the individual his inalienable rights; government was not empowered to invade, but, indeed, bound itself to preserve these rights.

The tension between absolute authority and individual liberty has been the theme of political history ever since. The political theory in Hobbes's social contract and the political theory in Locke's social contract present polarities which we find exemplified repeatedly in the course of the succeeding centuries.

From Hooker (the "judicious Hooker" Locke called him) Locke took over natural law ideas of the superiority of moral principles and their obligatory character. But Locke reformulated and "modernized" Hooker by moving to the concept of natural rights—inalienable natural rights. The individual, according to Locke, has a natural or inborn right to "life, liberty and estate." It is to the last, the right of private property, that he devotes much attention.

Like Hobbes, Locke posits a state of nature in which men have all the rights bestowed on them by nature. What they lack is the organization of a government. His "social contract" sets up the organization of a government pledged to preserve natural rights.

In Locke's version of the social contract, we have two steps. We first have a state of nature, which is not anarchic, however, as with Hobbes, but is guided by natural law. We then have a second step by which the majority gives its power to the government, which, however, must support the inalienable rights of the individual. Why Locke conceived the state of nature to be governed by natural law may perhaps be explained by the changed social ambience, in contrast to Hobbes's civil-war times, or perhaps by the prevalence of Christian morals in that society. If we are looking for logical nicety in Locke's treatise, we will not find it. Inalienable individual rights, for example, do not go with majority rule. But the United States Constitution managed this straddle. Locke's theory of private property, as that with which man mixes his personal labor, is a pat theory for his precommercial society, but his exaltation of private property, despite his outmoded theory, nonetheless remains prominent in our industrial society.

Locke's theory voiced ideas prevalent in his time, and they continued to be developed throughout the eighteenth and nineteenth centuries. Locke exemplified the resistance to absolutistic rule and the dawn of parliamentary government. The individual was liberated from absolutistic rule and was "endowed" with inalienable rights. Those rights enshrined for the rising middle class its acquisitive property-minded aims as well as its insistence on individual liberty. That Locke influenced Jefferson and the American Declaration of Independence and Constitution, there can be no doubt. It is obvious even without Jefferson's admission. The Lockean combination of inalienable rights of individual liberty and vested property still characterizes our electoral and Constitutional debates.

In the seventeenth century, the English common law—the cumulative rules about law as expressed and altered from case to case, from precedent to precedent—had already developed to such a point of acceptance that Lord Coke, the chief justice, was able to challenge King James I. When Coke was asked by the king (himself something of a philosopher) how the law proceeds, Coke replied, "By reason." The king indignantly rejoined: "But do I not have reason?" Whereupon Coke responded: not the "artificial reason" of the law by which your people are governed.

Coke was so confident in asserting the supremacy of the common law that he went the length of asserting the supremacy of the common law over acts of Parliament. In his opinion in *Bonham*'s case, he considers natural law ideas to be implicit in the common law: "When an act of parliament is against common right or reason . . . the common law will control it and adjudge such act to be void."

After the Glorious Revolution of 1688, in which Parliament was able forcibly to assert its power, the supremacy of Parliament was finally established. The supremacy of law merged with the supremacy of Parliament. There is no judicial review of legislation in England as in the United States. England has no written constitution and relies on Parliament to protect civil liberties simply in accordance with the long and deep English tradition.

When Blackstone in the eighteenth century put the common law of England into a comprehensive text, *Commentaries on the Laws of England,* he affirmed the supremacy of Parliament, which makes the laws. But Blackstone was not a rigorous or philosophical mind, and so he was not deterred from paradoxically echoing Cicero and Aquinas: "The law of nature being coeval with mankind and dictated by God himself is of course, superior in obligation to any other. It is binding over all the globe, in all countries and at all times; no human laws are of any validity contrary to this." He spoke of the common law as a kind of secondary natural law and the perfection of reason, commanding what is morally right and prohibiting what is morally wrong. Blackstone is one of the few authorities cited in the foundational opinions of Chief Justice John Marshall.

Once Chief Justice Marshall had established the prerogative of the Supreme Court to declare statutes unconstitutional, the Court employed natural law thinking to protect vested property rights against legislative incursions. In the nineteenth century, such natural law thinking provided resistance to much-needed social legislation which the Court invalidated but which we have since found entirely acceptable.

This trend continued until the furor over the Court's negation of the New Deal legislation to cope with the Depression in the 1930s.

The Court held to its obstructive resistance, over the strenuous dissents led by Justices Oliver Wendell Holmes and Louis D. Brandeis, until the threat of a "court-packing" scheme led Justice Owen Roberts to change the 5-4 vote in the Court. As a wag remarked, a switch in time saved nine.

After the Court had switched over to the Holmes-Brandeis position, concident with the appointment of new justices favorable to that approach, the Court held to "self-restraint" and stopped declaring unconstitutional ordinary legislative enactments designed to regulate economic activities. However, Chief Justice Harlan Stone developed a distinction which, though not hard-and-fast, holds that the Court must indeed exercise due restraint (and not freely go about invalidating economic statutes which a legislature deems necessary), but that a different standard should be used when the Court is considering a statute which impinges on the rights guaranteed in the Bill of Rights, of which the Court is the special guardian.

It is true that the Warren Court carried the implications of the Bill of Rights much further than the Stone Court, but Stone really made the vital break when in the *Jehovah's Witness* flag-salute cases he succeeded in getting the Court finally to agree (after first deciding the other way) that no one can be compelled to say something he does not believe.

Justice Felix Frankfurter, who dissented, was so determined to maintain judicial self-restraint, after the bitter New Deal experience, that he wanted to carry such restraint further, into the very Bill of Rights. This disposition to downgrade the Bill of Rights is evidenced also in Judge Learned Hand's characterization of these rights as mere admonitions.

The priority of personal over economic freedoms came to the fore again in the Senate deliberations over the Robert Bork appointment. This issue has come to the fore in our day in the nondiscrimination cases when affirmative action to amend discriminations comes into conflict with freedom of association and freedom of contract.

Many lawyers and the country at large applauded the Warren Court for bringing the country closer to its own ideals. Warren was able to get the entire Court to agree to *Brown v. Board of Education* overruling the earlier separate-but-equal directive for school facilities for blacks.

Other academic lawyers, though accepting the unanimous decision of *Brown v. Board of Education,* were disturbed at the creation of what they considered new rights not specified explicitly in the Constitution, like the right of privacy held to be implied by the spirit of the Bill of Rights in protecting the individual against legislative restrictions on personal liberty. The Bork hearings brought this issue to a head.

Chief Justice Earl Warren, in the spirit of natural law but with no reference to the metaphysics of natural law, would often ask counsel after the conclusion of a technical legal argument: but is it fair?

II

THE UTILITARIAN REVOLT AND LEGAL POSITIVISM

Introductory

We reach our own age with Jeremy Bentham's Utilitarianism and its correlative, legal positivism, developed by Bentham's colleague, John Austin.

Bentham was enraged by the muddleheaded natural law doctrine implicit in Blackstone's *Commentaries on the Laws of England*. When Bentham read in Blackstone that the case-by-case accumulations of English common law rules were a kind of "secondary natural law" and the "perfection of reason," he must have seen red. Apparently he decided he would demolish natural law then and there.

When a legislator is considering what position to take on a proposed piece of legislation, Bentham held he should be guided by nothing else than purely utilitarian considerations. That is to say, he should consider the consequences in minimizing misery or pains and maximizing happiness or pleasures.

Along with Bentham scuttling natural law, Austin identified law with the command of the state backed by its force. He considered the only law to be the positive or extant law; his theory is called "legal positivism."

Their younger colleague, John Stuart Mill, made the incisive distinction, which guided my analysis of the background of the concept of natural law, between the laws of nature, which scientists discern and *de*scribe, and laws as standards which *pre*scribe our conduct. Not nature, but only humans, can decide what is good or bad.

Mill went beyond Bentham in stressing liberty, as well as security or order. "The only freedom which deserves the name is that of pursuing our own good in our own way." Such freedom notably included freedom of speech so as to enable minorities to aspire to majority position through the appeal of their thought, thus avoiding the tyranny of a majority.

In this section we present the thought of Bentham, Austin, and Mill, followed, in the next section, by Holmes's pursuance of their thought in the United States with a pragmatic twist which inspired the movement of Legal Realism, which is the climactic outcome.

The radical break away from "reason" originated not with Bentham but with David Hume. He was not a legal philosopher, but he emancipated philosophy from its age-old reliance on "reason." Our goals are determined not by reason, he said, but by what he called our "passions." Reason, he said, is but the "slave of passions." We can utilize reason as a way of helping us to achieve whatever we wish or desire. Our reason or intelligence is not a source of wisdom about life, but is simply a method to be used to gain our ends.

2

Jeremy Bentham (1748–1832): The Shift to Consequences

In the eighteenth century, English law was not taught at any university, and lawyers were trained practically at the famous Inns of Court. William Blackstone, an unsuccessful practitioner, was frustrated in his effort to secure the post at Oxford University teaching Roman law. He persuaded the university to permit him to teach a course in English law to the sons of the squires who wanted to know something about the law without becoming lawyers. This course was a huge success. Soon his lectures were reduced to notes by some of his students, who began to bootleg them. Blackstone then decided to write them up himself in a comprehensive book, which he called *Commentaries on the Laws of England*. Blackstone had an essentially conservative turn of mind and he possessed little logical acumen. The result was a book which contained a great many rules and details but which was not at all critical or sophisticated in its philosophic underpinning. Blackstone thought that the English law of his day had reached the "perfection of reason." He swallowed natural law theory whole and he referred to the English common law as "a secondary law of nature." He defined the law as commanding what is good and prohibiting what is wrong. It is clear that he meant morally good and morally wrong. That being the case, the law could be neither criticized nor improved. One can imagine how such a position would have aroused the ire of a sharply critical mind like Jeremy Bentham.

Bentham lit into Blackstone with a fury. A small part of his attack was published while Blackstone was bringing out the several volumes of his *Commentaries*. Bentham modestly called it *A Fragment on Government*. His more vigorous and extensive attack on Blackstone did not see the light of day until over a century later—in the 1920s, with the title *Comment on the Commentaries*. (Bentham did not care if everything he wrote got published.) Bentham was disgusted not only with Blackstone's confusion of thought but with Blackstone's book's naive or opaque remoteness from the actual legal practices of the day.

Bentham was a dedicated legal theorist and reformer. Educated at Oxford and at Lincoln's Inn, he was admitted to the bar, but he never practiced law. Having inherited a modest income, he resolved to concentrate on law as a subject of intellectual study and philosophic analysis. He wanted to develop a sound and modern theory of jurisprudence and, on the basis of this enlightenment, to devote himself to a reform of the law and its archaic institutions. Though he found himself involved in more basic ethical theory, his chief influence has been on jurisprudence, and he and his followers have been enormously influential in the jettisoning of many clumsy, cumbersome, expensive, ambiguous, and cruel procedures and laws. He has been a strong force in the efforts to make our legal system simpler and more humane, clearer and more coherent.

In 1789, the same year as the adoption of our Constitution, he brought out his masterpiece, *Introduction to the Principles of Morals and Legislation*. A sequel, in which he anticipated his colleague, Austin, entitled *The Limits of Jurisprudence Defined*, was not published until 1945.

Blackstone made the greater popular splurge in America. In the book-poor colonies, his was the only compendious volume on the English common law (which had been "received" here as our law). John Marshall's father bought John a set. Abraham Lincoln studied law from Blackstone.

But Bentham had a terrific impact on thoughtful minds and has had widespread influence among legal scholars and reformers. Many philosophers and professors of law in this country and in England avow themselves to be Benthamites. It was through his colleague, John Austin, that his legal theory was cogently elaborated. Its influence in America increased incalculably through the prestige and eloquent exposition of Justice Oliver Wendell Holmes, Jr., who gave it a pragmatic twist.

Bentham was the founder of the Utilitarian school of philosophy with its principle of utility: consider the consequences in terms of pleasure and pain; to quote his exact words: "that principle which approves or disapproves of every action whatsoever, according to the tendency it has to augment or diminish the happiness of the party whose interest is in question." It may be the happiness of the individual or the happiness of the community. During his lifetime, his influence spread through a society which the Utilitarians established, through a journal they published, and through University College, which he started in London. It was there that John Austin lectured as the first professor of jurisprudence. These lectures were incorporated in his pivotal book, *The Province of Jurisprudence Determined,* which marked the turning point from natural law to what came to be known as legal positivism.

The name *Utilitarianism* comes from Bentham's basic premise, the principle of utility. In a later footnote, he tells us he would have preferred to call it the principle of happiness. (His philosophy was so heterodox a departure that the Utilitarians were also sometimes known as the Philosophic Radicals.) Happiness is what is good. What is bad is pain or suffering. Thus one state of affairs is better than another if it produces a greater balance of pleasure over pain. That state of affairs is best which produces the greatest balance of happiness over suffering.

When we have to decide between two courses of action, the way to go about it is to consider the consequences of each course. We should weigh the pleasures and pains involved in each course for all the persons involved. Bentham's was not an individual hedonism but, as it is sometimes termed, a "universal" hedonism. His basic assumption is that every man counts as one. But since the greatest happiness of *all* is utopian, he settled on the well-known slogan: the greatest happiness of the greatest number.

What irked him in Blackstone was Blackstone's reliance on both the doctrine of natural law and the doctrine of the social contract. Bentham firmly—even derisively—rejected both doctrines.

Bentham was an unremitting rationalist who would have no truck with any theory which he could not accept as entirely reasonable.

He thought natural law was entirely useless because it did not enable us to distinguish between good laws and bad laws. How could it do so when it took the position that it could not recognize any laws as bad because it held that any such putative laws are not laws at all?

He thought social contract theory was fantastic because, rationalist that he was, he took the idea of social contract literally, and as such it was a myth pure and simple. How could a mere myth be the basis for the existence of government and a citizen's obligation? Truth, he said, had no use for such "rattles."

The same line of reasoning led to his rejection of any such notion as a moral law or moral laws, which to him were not really "laws" at all since laws required the sanction of the state. Anything not enforced by the state could not be considered a "law." He ridiculed the so-called moral laws which men had accepted as immutable and which were supposed to tell us which actions were good and which actions were bad. For Bentham it was impossible to characterize any action without considering its consequences. There is no immutable prior standard. To make any such supposition was for Bentham the basic error in previous moral theory. This obsolete moral theory, he argued, was at the basis of the misguidance of legislators and all of the inconsistencies and archaisms in the law. The legislator assumed that he had a grasp of these absolute principles which he must follow. This kind of intuitive conviction that he knew these eternal moral principles was nothing more than what Bentham caustically labeled "ipsedixitism."

One by one, he shows all the traditional systems of ethics to be disguises for "do this because I want it." They are either arbitrary or ascetic. It was for this reason that the criminal code contained many offenses for which men were punished even though the offender had not caused anyone to suffer. His prime example was the so-called sexual offenses. By the same token, there were other actions which caused great suffering but which were left unpunished. And the punishment might be too severe or too slight in relation to the suffering caused.

Though Bentham won international fame during his lifetime and was made an honorary citizen of the new French Republic, he was not deterred from dismissing natural rights as "nonsense on stilts." The French Declaration of the Rights of Man and the Citizen, as well as the American Declaration of Independence, he condemned as spurious. Their spuriousness lay in their confusion between *is* and *ought,* actual and ideal, fact and value.

Take the statement in the Declaration of Independence, based on Locke's natural rights theory, that men have certain inalienable rights—rights which cannot be taken away from them by the government. Bentham points out that this assertion is the statement of an ideal. It asserts that men should have certain inalienable rights and that men are all equal in this respect. If men were in fact equal in possessing such natural rights, there would be no need for a Declaration of Independence—followed by a revolution. Thus the statement that all men are created equal really means that all men ought to be treated as equals, but that the government is not treating them as equals, and therefore they must protest.

So far, so good. But Bentham goes further. He proceeds to argue that if we construe the doctrine of natural rights to mean what a government ought to do, the doctrine is untenable. If we take the doctrine that men's liberties and property are beyond governmental tampering at its face value, it would mean, realistically speaking, that the government could not imprison anyone for crimes or tax property to support the government's activities. It would be impossible to have any government or system of laws which did not impinge on men's liberties and property. Indeed, every law is a restraint on someone's liberty.

The difficulty with his position is that he was concerned solely with security through law—with an orderly society. Unlike his younger Utilitarian successor, John Stuart Mill, he did not have his eye fixed on liberty. In order that a man might have individual liberty, there must be quite definite and stringent limitations on the power of the state to enact law. In the framework of our own Constitution we have placed these liberties into the Bill of Rights and the "due process' clause, and we put these guarantees against overweening legislation into the keeping of our Supreme Court. The Supreme Court can wield only a moral influence when a Court decision runs against the government and orders the government to refrain from some action. In Bentham's hardheaded approach, that kind of influence could not be called law. We must remember that, in his day, our Revolution and the French Revolution had just begun. Bentham would probably be astonished to see how well our Constitutional protection of civil liberties has worked out.

In Bentham's light, it seemed ridiculous to say that a legislator is under a duty not to make certain laws. For Bentham, "duty" was equated with what one can be punished for not doing. And it seemed to him absurd to say that the legislators could be punished for making certain laws. To him the legislators were the governors, and they were the supreme lawmakers. If we say that natural law imposes a duty upon the legislature to refrain from making certain laws, then that would mean for Bentham that we were talking about some kind of duty which was not a legal duty—not a duty for which one could be punished. In that case it could be nothing more than a moral duty.

He had no objection to talking about "moral duties." A moral duty is not unimportant or negligible, but it is simply not a legal duty and should not be considered an integral part of law—law as coercive and leading to a governmental penalty. Such a moral duty is not the same thing as a legal restraint. It is not law at all. The only justification for law is the principle of utility. The only justification for restraining anyone would be, after weighing the consequences in the balance, to avoid pain to other persons, to maximize happiness, and to minimize suffering.

All of which is not to say that moral duties do not have some political significance or that they can be ignored. The legislator cannot wield the principle of utility like a cudgel, paying no heed to what various persons may consider to be their moral duties or, indeed, what he himself may consider to be his duty. The legislator would not usually care to—or indeed dare to—go beyond what public opinion would bear.

If we wish to think of these moral duties as, in some sense, religious duties, then the sanction for their violation would be punishment by God. There would still be no justification for considering them law—a breach of which is punished by the government.

In polar contrast with the expounders of a concept of natural law, Bentham insisted on the essential distinguishability between law and morality. They have no necessary connection. Their intersection is purely accidental. If we ask what connection should obtain between them, we would have to find the answer by invoking the criterion of utility.

The state has no separate status or identity with a will or aim of its own. The state is simply a human contrivance to enable man to pursue happiness.

Bentham's revolt led not only to the analytic jurisprudence of John Austin, which we are next to examine, but also to the later developments in America of "sociological jurisprudence" and "legal realism."

His revolt cast a long beam into contemporary legal reconstructions. His influence is not exhausted in the central theme elaborated by Austin: the separation of morals and law and the designation of law as a province of its own. By his radical shift to *human consequences,* Bentham taught us that the meaning of legal concepts cannot be found only in their relation to other concepts. He opened the door to the exploration of these consequences in relation to the potentialities of the social sciences of economics, sociology, psychology, and anthropology as materials for an understanding of law.

In giving great emphasis to obedience to law as vital to law, he flagged the need for general legal education (such as my book aspires to be) and to the function of dramatic legal penalties (which may explain the persistence of the death penalty).

He urged that the real impact or efficacy of law lay in its enforcement rather than in the severity of the punishment, and that the problem of enforcing the law is also a problem in lessening the social conditions which lead to lawbreaking. This twin emphasis attends our present-day war on drugs.

To dispel the inherited ambiguities, he urged a "functional" approach which begins with our common experience, and he showed how a legal "right" becomes a *function* of a judge's behavior in making real the benefits and enjoyment of a legal right. Thus he leads into Holmes's pragmatic theory that law is a prediction of what a judge will do.

From Bentham to Austin to Holmes is the triple play of Anglo-American jurisprudence.

3

John Austin (1790–1859): The Separation of Law and Morality

Let us recall that we are in a direct line from Hobbes's central emphasis on the power of the sovereign as we now come to John Austin's grounding of law upon that keystone. By the nineteenth century, the modern national state had taken shape, with an active legislature as the obvious source of law: one statute after another. The Utilitarian philosophy had already moved toward an influential position as the emergent, reformist liberalism.

The precursor of the Utilitarian movement, David Hume, had sharply formulated the philosophic distinction in ethical theory between *is* and *ought,* between fact and value, the cornerstone upon which Austin built.

In a famous passage, Hume tells us how puzzled he became when he read in philosophic treatises a transition not from "is" to "is not," as one would expect, but from "is" to "ought not." How can one move validly in this way from fact to value? asked Hume. No, we must make a clean-cut distinction between *is* and *should;* they are two different things. The famous passage from Hume's *Treatise of Human Nature* reads as follows:

> In every system of morality which I have hitherto met with, I have always remarked, that the author proceeds for some time in the ordinary way of reasoning, and establishes the being of a God or makes observations concerning human affairs: when of a sudden I am surprised to find, that instead of the usual copulations of propositions, *is* and *is not,* I meet with no proposition that is not connected with an *ought,* or an *ought not*. This change is imperceptible; but it is, however, of the last

consequence. For as this *ought* or *ought not,* expresses some new relation or affirmation, it is necessary that it should be observed or explained; and at the same time that a reason should be given, for what seems altogether inconceivable, how this new relation can be a deduction from others, which are entirely different from it.

Commenting on this passage, the distinguished contemporary natural law philosopher A. F. d'Entrèves observes:

I doubt that the main objection to natural law thinking could be put forward with more clarity and cogency than in this classic statement. It is the objection to what in the language of the modern semanticists is called the passage from the indicative to the imperative mood, an objection, one must admit, based on a perfectly accurate description of what natural law theorists are ultimately after.

Austin now set about to separate the law as it is from the law as it ought to be. To make this aseptic distinction was precisely what the natural law tradition declined to do. In that tradition, as we saw, the *is* and the *ought* are fused, and the existing law is required to connect reflexively with the moral oughts. Like Bentham, Austin rejected the natural law approach and developed his theory of law exclusively upon an analysis of the existent legal system—its terms and structures. He erected a formidable edifice of theoretical justification.

Austin abandoned a career in the army and devoted himself, like Bentham, to law, not as a professional practice, but as a cynosure of philosophic interest and analysis. He prepared very carefully for his microscopic analyses, published under the title *The Province of Jurisprudence Determined*. He established firmly a well-delineated and insulated discipline, the special and distinctive province of jurisprudence. He drew its boundary lines, sharply distinguishing it from other subjects. He drew a detailed map of its terrain.

We move with Austin to an end point of a progression which began in earliest times with law, religion, and morality being indistinguishable, to law theologically defended in the Middle Ages, to law philosophically grounded in the seventeenth century, to the groundwork of law as the separate province of jurisprudence, marked off decisively from other disciplines, including ethics. It was to be a science of jurisprudence, like other theoretical sciences, spawned in an age of science.

Austin's method is to make a punctilious logical and linguistic analysis of the way the word *law* is commonly used and to distinguish it from what he thinks is the only correct and proper way to use the word *law*. He follows with an equally painstaking verbal analysis of the structure of an existing legal system.

The subject matter of jurisprudence he called "positive law" and his theory is aptly known as "legal positivism." By "positive law," to put it summarily, he meant the rules set forth by political superiors in the state. There is no connection with the philosophical positivism of the nineteenth-century French philosopher, Auguste Comte, though doubtless Austin could have subscribed to Comte's suggestion that the movement of Western philosophic thought had been from a theological stage through a metaphysical stage to a positivistic or scientific stage.

The term *positive law,* the subject matter of jurisprudence, is distinguished by him from other uses of the term *law*. To him positive law was law, as he said, "simply and strictly so-called." Other uses of the term *law* were thus to be understood only in terms of their resemblance to this exclusively correct use of the term *law,* strictly so-called or, as he also puts it, "properly so-called." He proposes to distinguish every other use of the term *law* by reference to positive law which is law, strictly and properly denominated.

Before we get to positive law, he says, let us consider what we mean by a law generally—in its broadest and most comprehensive sense. Speaking thus generally, he conceives of a law as a "rule"— a rule laid down by A, who has power over B, for the guidance of B. Now, says Austin, in this large sense, we speak about laws which are set by men for other men. In the political entity of the state, such rules are "positive law." We also find persons speaking of laws set by God for men. Such rules, he says, are called "law" only by analogy to positive law (law strictly and properly so-called). You see he starts with positive law and looks back at theological rules which are then to be called law, for him, only by analogy to positive law (law strictly so-called). We have seen in our historical survey that the earlier approach was to envelope and to appraise state-enforced law in the broader moral (or moral-religious) perspective of the natural law approach, in which state-enforced law finds its niche.

These laws set by God to men, says Austin, have been styled "natural law." But, demurs Austin, why use so ambiguous and misleading an expression? Let us call a spade a spade, he as much as says, and let us use the plain characterization "law of God." God's law is not within the "province of jurisprudence determined," and so there is no need to consider it further in the province of jurisprudence determined.

Alf Ross, a present-day Scandinavian legal positivist, leaves no doubt that he would also dismiss "the will of God," along with "absolute reason" and alleged "insights," or any other transcendent or metaphysical source for the validity of law. "Natural law," he writes, "seeks the absolute, the eternal, that shall make of law something more than the handiwork of human beings and exempt the legislator from the pains and responsibility of decision." Ross would push all metaphysical speculation "into oblivion along with other myths and legends of the childhood of civilization." For "experience shows that the doctrines men have built on these sources, far from being eternal and immutable, have changed according to time, place and person."

Scientific laws—laws governing physical bodies—says Austin, when considered from the baseline of positive law, are called laws only metaphorically. And when we use the term *law* metaphorically in this way, we muddy up the waters of jurisprudence. For people think positive laws and scientific laws are the same thing, but scientific laws are called laws only by grace of a metaphorical extension of the correct use of the term *law*. Thus it is that the positive law, which is the province of jurisprudence appropriately determined, is set apart.

What about laws (or rules) set by men for men when the former are not political superiors? We speak of such rules, generally, as rules of morality. But the term *morality* embraces both morality as it is (regardless of its merits) and morality as it should be. Thus to avoid this confusion in the realm of morality he uses the term *positive morality*. Morality *as it is* must be singled out and covered by the term *positive morality*.

I should pause to warn my reader that I am now streamlining his analysis, as his distinctions and subdistinctions have begun to reach a point of subtle overrefinement which evokes sympathy for his sweetheart, who complained that his love letters read like a mortgage indenture.

Since Austin uses the term *law* interchangeably with *rule*, he feels called upon to analyze the essentials of a rule—that is to say, a law.

Every law is a command. The term *command* is the key to his jurisprudence, which is usually called the "command theory of law."

As though by anticipation, Thomas Aquinas had already sought to answer his own contemporaries who spoke of law as commands of the sovereign. Speaking of the jurist who contended that "Whatsoever pleaseth the sovereign has the force of law," Thomas observed that it is true that the law commands. But command belongs to reason. And the law pertains to reason. In Thomas's words:

> But in order that the volition of what is commanded may have the nature of law it needs to be in accord with some rule of reason. And in this sense is to be understood the saying that the will of the sovereign has the force of law; or otherwise the sovereign's will would savor of lawlessness rather than of law.

To Austin, law emanates from the sovereign and not from "reason."

As Austin takes apart the term *command*, he is aware that he is taxing the patience of his readers. He expresses the hope that they will bear with him cheerfully—or at least resignedly. He begs us to appreciate the difficulty of his task in explaining the elements of this new science of jurisprudence. He is sorry, he says, to be driven into awkward circumlocutions as he seeks to define these elements.

What then are the ideas contained in the term *command?*

Austin seeks to get down to the simplest possible terms as he locates the meaning of a command in the wish (or desire) which some men express to control the conduct of other men.

We see encapsulated in a command three things: a wish (or desire), the expression of the wish, and what will happen to someone who does not comply with the wish (what "evil" he will be made to suffer, as Austin puts it).

If you express a wish that I shall do something, and if you will inflict some evil (or pain) on me if I do not do it, the expression of your wish is a command. (If you are a political superior it is plain that the evil inflicted in that context would usually be imprisonment or the exaction of money.) A command differs from the ordinary expression of a wish (or desire) precisely in that the person to whom it is directed is exposed to such evil from the directing party, if there is not compliance.

When I am liable to such evil from you, we may say I am "bound" by your command, or I am "obliged" by it, or, as it is often put, that I am under a duty to obey it. If I do not comply with your wish, despite the evil in prospect for me, I am said to disobey your command or to violate the duty which the command imposes. Thus duty is correlated with command, and command is correlated with duty. Each implies the other. When you command, I am under a duty to obey.

Thus, in summary, the ideas contained in the term *command* are (1) a wish by A that B shall do something (or forebear); (2) an expression of A's wish—as through words; (3) an evil incurred by B imposed by A.

The use of the word *evil* seems quaint to us today to describe what we should call the sanction of the law—what happens to one who disobeys. Indeed Austin makes the very suggestion that the term *sanction* be used to describe the evil incurred if a duty is broken.

If we abstract the evil (or sanction) entirely away from the command and look at it separately, we may call it the "punishment."

Thus a command is an order backed by the threat that some sanction will be imposed to enforce the order; and that if the implied (and correlated) duty to obey the command does not follow, the punishment will ensue.

Austin has furnished us with much of the vocabulary with which we communicate with each other about legal matters today.

Austin seems to be thinking chiefly of the criminal law—and he is thinking in terms of the emergence of such law from the legislature (as the sovereign or political superior). To think of law in terms of the sanction or punishment is to think of it in terms of the criminal law. To consider law as essentially a command from a superior would also come naturally to one who had served as an officer in the military.

We may now pick up his technical terms—duty and sanction—and instead of speaking colloquially of wishes and their expression, we may use the terms which are more familiar in legal discourse. We may now speak of duty and sanction as integrally tied up with command.

The expression is the *command*.
The evil is the *sanction*.
The chance of incurring the evil is the *duty*.

As you might suppose, "analytical" jurisprudents like Austin and those who follow him today are admirers and exemplars of the rigor of the discipline of formal logic. Indeed Austin praises the study and the use of logic for its precision, distinctness, and brevity. Employing the terminology of logic, he describes his analysis of command into its threefold character as one in which each of the three terms signifies the same notion, but each of them denotes a different part of the notion while connoting the rest of it.

But we are not by any means through with our dissection of the key concept: command.

There are two kinds of commands: (1) general commands which are laws (or rules), which pertain to a whole class of acts and oblige us generally (like statutory laws condeming homicide), and (2) particular commands which pertain to a specific or individual act (or forbearance), as for example, the judge's sentencing of a convicted murderer.

The thrust of this twofold distinction is now clear. The legislature issues a general command (the law or rule); the judge issues a particular command. The legislature prohibits murder and commands the type of punishment. This is general. The judge commands that the killer shall get life imprisonment. The judge is acting in accordance with the general command of the legislature, which is the law (or rule). The legislature is speaking of acts generally of a certain class: homicides. The judge speaks of a specific determination: this killer and his punishment.

In the light of this breakdown, we may now define a law more closely. A law, "properly so-called," is a command which obliges persons in general to acts (or forebearances) of a certain class. (It obliges persons to engage, we may say, in a "course of conduct.") Laws proceed from a "superior" and oblige (or bind) an "inferior."

Austin feels constrained to take the mystery out of the terms *superior* and *inferior*.

By "superiority" he says he means "might." That is to say, the power to inflict evil, and to force others—through fear of the evil—to act in accordance with the wishes of the superior. Thus the sovereign is the superior of the citizen.

But the sovereign is not absolute. Let us refer to the sovereign as the governor. The governor is superior to the governed. The power of the governor can force the governed to comply. But the governed are also the governor's superior, as he is checked from abuse of his power by the fear of arousing the power of their resistance. The relation is reciprocal.

The same is true of the relation between the legislator and the judge. The judge must follow the law which emanates from the legislature, which is sovereign. Thus the legislator is superior to the judge. But the legislator is also a citizen, and in this role he is inferior to the judge, for the judge can enforce the law against him as a citizen.

We now see how superiority is implied in the concept of command. For superiority lies in the power of enforcing compliance with one's wish. The elements of a command are the expression of a wish with the power to enforce it.

Austin then makes a very significant addition, which he takes for granted but which is of the utmost importance to any sociologically minded critic. The law comprises not only the command of the sovereign, but also the *habit of obedience*. The American pragmatists, James and Dewey, made much of the importance of recognizing habit.

4

John Stuart Mill (1806–1873): Liberty

In his influential essay "On Liberty," written over a century ago, John Stuart Mill wrote one of the most eloquent and seminal documents of modern society. He supplemented Bentham's emphasis on security with a fervent defense of individual liberty. The question he confronted was: What does it mean to be a free man in a free society?

John Stuart Mill had been privately educated by his own father, James Mill, who was a colleague and disciple of Bentham. Young Mill was uniquely educated to become a Utilitarian. He was extremely precocious and, before reaching adolescence, he had mastered Greek and was reading Plato. As a result of this inimitable education, he was virtually a whole generation ahead of his contemporaries. The story of his development is fascinatingly related in his *Autobiography*. He also wrote on logic and political economy, making substantial contributions in both fields. All the while, he worked at an executive post in the East India Company and, for a time, he was a member of Parliament. His essay on "The Emancipation of Women" anticipates much of the women's lib movement.

He goes beyond Bentham in treating each individual person, not as an opaque integer, but as a unique personality, with the capacity to develop distinctive potentialities in ever higher degrees of individual development.

He goes beyond Bentham also in distinguishing certain qualities as better than others. It did not satisfy him to accept the notion that whatever gave a person pleasure was satisfactory. He would never have thought that pushpin (a child's game) was as good as poetry, as Bentham suggests. He would rather be Socrates dissatisfied, he avowed, than a fool or a pig satisfied.

At the center of his essay "On Liberty" is the primacy of freedom of thought and its expression in speech or print. It is not simply that we run the risk of suppressing truth. We should positively and intrinsically appreciate the efforts of those who combat our opinions, he urged, because they force us to establish our views on sound grounds or to modify them. If one man differed from all the rest of us, we would no more be justified in shutting him up than he would in shutting us up.

Nor should we ever permit a majority to channel rigidly the conduct of the rest of us. Today's minority should be free to become tomorrow's majority. The given majority is so overwhelming in its pressures that we must be everlastingly vigilant to resist its stultifications.

He was also concerned to keep society open to individual initiative as the key to progress, both material and moral.

The greatest danger of the times, he thought, was the fear men have of being regarded as eccentric. So basic did he regard complete freedom of thought and individual expression that he thought that the very well-being of society depended upon it. By the well-being of society, he meant its culture or civilization, its educational or rational development.

For individuals to be free in a free society meant that the one and only justification for interference with an individual's liberty is to prevent harm to others. The law is not justified in curbing and penalizing anyone either for his own good or because someone thinks it would be wiser or better for him to behave in some prescribed way.

The prestigious Wolfenden Report, rendered in England in the 1960s, took the Millian position that there is a sphere of private morality which is none of the law's business. What consenting adults do in private is their own business. The Model Penal Code of the American Law Institute proceeds largely on the same premise. The agitations in our own day over the rights of homosexuals, for example, to be free of governmental punishments stem from Mill's libertarian principle. But, as Joel Feinberg has said, we are not a "utilitarian society (as yet)."

Mills' views made great headway in enlightened scholarly and professional circles. Then a challenge to his view was forcefully made in the 1960s by Lord Devlin in his book, *The Enforcement of Morality*. He argues that *any* action which might *upset* society could become the law's business. He argues that it is the sense of disgust of the man-on-the-bus which should be the index to legal enforcement of morality. A doughty rejoinder to Devlin was made by H. L. A. Hart in his book, *Law, Liberty and Morality*. What a comedown, says Hart, from law as "God's will" or man's "reason" to find its source in the sick stomach of the man-on-the-bus. Hart is prepared, however, to concede a degree of paternalism to the modern state, as when it requires us to save money, whether we want to or not, through social security taxes to forfend against destitution in our old age. Hart thinks Mill exaggerated the rational capacity of the average man to make cool and reflective decisions about all matters which concern him.

Isaiah Berlin, a present-day champion of Mill, points out, that libertarians, like Locke and Mill, concede that man's freedom to act must be limited by law, but they also hold that there must be some area of personal freedom which cannot be violated under any circumstances. Berlin is at pains to make very clear that liberty so conceived, while it is not everything a man needs or desires, is what is to be meant by liberty. He does not want liberty to be confused with equality or justice or happiness or whatever. Mill, like Locke, had a sufficiently optimistic view of human nature to believe that it was possible to preserve a large area for a man's private life and development, which he can handle himself, and which the state must not invade. Mill, like Locke, thought one could so live in society without sacrificing the harmony or progress of society. This concept of liberty means liberty *"from."* It means absence of legal interference if we are not hurting anyone. "The only freedom which deserves the name is that of pursuing our own good in our own way," wrote Mill.

Berlin contrasts this "negative", Millian, freedom with what he objects to as "positive" freedom, which derives from the theory that government has the right to interfere with the lives of men, so as to direct their lives with the aim of increasing their positive freedom by making them do what they would really want to do if they knew better. For those who hold to the preservation of Mill's negative liberty, the proponents of so-called positive liberty are merely rationalizing, in the name of freedom, an excuse for a measure of tyrannical dictatorship which would destroy a truly free society.

Mill believed in democracy. In order that a democratic government might function auspiciously, he thought it was essential that citizens had to be educated and had to learn how to be tolerant of the views of others and how to modify their self-interest for the general good of society. It was impossible for a democracy to learn these lessons unless the tendency to exalt the majority was tempered so that individuals and minorities were not overridden and repressed. He foresaw the potentialities in a democracy for majority tyranny through the power to manipulate public opinion. Our greatest safeguard, he argued, lay in the development of individuals strong enough to enable us to resist these enormous pressures.

To trace clearly the line I am developing from Austin to Holmes to Legal Realism, I might have omitted Mill. But Mill is highly significant for a phase of development which I touched on in the section on natural law, where I discuss civil liberties under our Constitution. I am not dwelling on Constitutional law in this book, as I am telling a different story here. But we should note that though Holmes is at the apex of our story in the development of law proper, so to say (and not the branch of law known as Constitutional law), Holmes as a Supreme Court justice did express the same solicitude as Mill for the liberties safeguarded in our Bill of Rights.

When the Supreme Court excogitated a "right of privacy" in the "penumbra" of our liberty, the Court was giving dynamic expression to the advanced thinking of Mill already endorsed in England in the Wolfenden Report. By setting his face against it, Judge Bork met a stumbling block in the Senate confirmation hearings. In his subsequent book, *The Tempting of America,* Bork discloses that he is operating from different moral premises.

III

THE AMERICAN FRUITIONS

5

Thomas Jefferson (1743–1826): Equality

In discussing Jefferson, we again diverge from our main line, but we disgress to round out the picture. The most philosophical statesman the United States has ever had was Thomas Jefferson. Third president of the United States, he preferred his tombstone to read: author of the Declaration of Independence and the Virginia statute of religious liberty, and founder of the University of Virginia. He was most proud, not of the offices he held, but of the blows he struck for political, religious, and intellectual freedom. He was so versatile in his erudition that President John F. Kennedy used to say that the best conversation in the White House occurred when President Jefferson sat down to dine alone.

Jefferson is the social philosopher of American democracy. Born in Virginia, he was admitted to the Virginia bar, but early became engrossed in public affairs. Before long he stood out as a leader of the opposition to British oppression. He gave preeminent literary expression to the ferments which led to the Revolution. His authorship of the Declaration of Independence was preceded by one year by his *Declaration of the Causes and Necessities for Taking Up Arms*. Active in the Continental Congress, he also served as governor of Virginia and succeeded Benjamin Franklin as our ambassador to France in 1785. Later he became secretary of state in Washington's first cabinet. He became disenchanted with the Federalist domination of the government and Alexander Hamilton's plutocratic sympathies, scorning Hamilton's view that men can only be governed by a "rod." A strong champion of the civil liberties in the Bill of Rights, he bitterly opposed the Alien and Sedition Acts. He was eventually elected president in 1801. When he retired to his home in Monticello in 1809, he devoted his remaining years to a continuation of his studies and the founding of the University of Virginia.

Besides his political and literary gifts, he was a model of a Renaissance man, for he was an outstanding architect, a contributor to the science of paleontology, and an accomplished violinist.

Although Jefferson read widely, there is no question that his thought was channeled in the English tradition of philosophy; John Locke was a great influence upon his thought. On his wall, he placed pictures of three English philosophers: Locke, Frances Bacon, and Isaac Newton. One day he was visited by Hamilton who asked who they were. Jefferson responded that they were the three greatest men who ever lived. (To which Hamilton retorted that Julius Caesar was the greatest man who ever lived.) Locke was influenced by Newtonian science, and Bacon supplemented Locke by his emphasis on experimentation. John Dewey, in this line of development in our own time, often referred back to Bacon.

More than any thinker in England itself, Jefferson is the flower of Locke's philosophy. Though Locke's treatise may not have influenced the peaceful English Revolution of 1688, there is no doubt that Jefferson's writings, so indebted to Locke, did influence the American Revolution.

Jefferson thought that Locke's doctrine of natural rights (which Thomas Paine called the rights of man) had come to be achieved in his time as the rights of all men. He saw the French Revolution as a sequel to the American Revolution, remarking that the "appeal to the rights of man, which had been made in the United States, was taken up by France." Jefferson thought these revolutions were the watershed of history. He thought that at long last the lives of men throughout the world would be, as he put it, "finally and greatly ameliorated."

In religious orientation, he admired Christian ethics and accepted the widespread religious convention of his day known as deism. In contrast to traditional theism, the deist held that, though God was the creator of the world, he was not its governor. This belief explains why in writing the Declaration of Independence he spoke of our being endowed with inalienable rights by our creator. His conviction that these are human rights of all men is memorialized in the familiar affirmations of the Declaration of Independence:

> We hold these truths to be self-evident: that all men are created equal, that they are endowed by their Creator with certain unalienable rights, that among these are life, liberty and the pursuit of happiness; that to secure these rights, governments are instituted among men, deriving their just powers from the consent of the governed; that whenever any form of government becomes destructive of these ends, it is the right of the people to alter or abolish it.

Instead of the word *self-evident* he had originally written "sacred and undeniable," but Benjamin Franklin induced him to use the more secular expression, "self-evident."

Jefferson once later explained that by "self-evident" he meant nothing more than "the common sense of the subject."

Jefferson had also originally written in but expunged the words "inherent and" before the word "unalienable," which he misspelled.

It will be recalled that Locke's enumeration had been "life, liberty, health and property." The ones listed by Jefferson are not exhaustive but are described as "among" these rights. That he reflected Locke's concept of natural rights is obvious enough. Indeed, Jefferson said that he offered "no sentiment which had never been expressed before." One of Jefferson's contemporaries remarked that it was the Declaration which introduced him to the doctrine of civil liberties as taught by Locke. (It was Eleanor Roosevelt who introduced the term *human* rights at the U.N. to replace Paine's rights *of man*.)

Though Jefferson derived the "just powers" of government from the consent of the governed, there is no reference to the social contract. In the wording of the Declaration, no ruler stands out over and against the people as an independent party to any supposed contract. Men are born equal. Period!

In Jefferson's theory, the men of every generation are free to judge for themselves whether to maintain the government. The government is not a party to a contract which it may try to enforce against the people. The government consists of functionaries who are provisionally entrusted with power by the people. It is indeed a government of the people, by the people, for the people. Since there has been no "original contract," no generation can be said to bind its successor generation. We are not to be ruled by the dead hand of the past. Jefferson found the basis for the new government, he said, not in our Constitution but "merely in the spirit of our people." Since a new generation comes along every twenty years, Jefferson contemplated that there could be an overhauling every twenty years to receive renewed popular authorization. He thought of these overhaulings as thunderstorms which clear the air. "The spirit of resistance is so valuable on certain occasions," he wrote, "that I wish it to be always kept alive."

Jefferson posited equality, just as Locke had done, in the state of nature. As Bentham perceived, this premise is the statement of an ideal. It is an expression of the American dream. It is a refusal to acquiesce in prevailing inequalities. It is a dedication to the realization of a continuous goal.

Jefferson assumed that men were equal at the starting line and that an auspicious education could advance them; the lack of education could impede them.

The logic of the Declaration would have compelled renunciation of slavery. Jefferson wanted to insert such a renunciation. He was forced to retreat by the intransigence of southern delegates. He tells us in his autobiography that the clause "reprobating the enslaving the inhabitants of Africa, was struck out in complaisance to South Carolina and Georgia, who had never attempted to restrain the importation of slaves, and who, on the contrary, still wished to continue it." He was not unmindful of some reluctance in some of the other states as well, for he added: "Our northern brethren also, I believe, felt a little tender under those censures; for though their people had very few slaves themselves, yet they had been pretty considerable carriers of them to others."

As Lincoln said: "The principles of Jefferson are definitions and axioms of free society." Jefferson was not an academician or professional philosopher. He wrote no jurisprudential treatises. But his thought served to form the mind of America. We continue to return to his inspiration as recurrently we recover our faith.

Certain aspects of Jefferson's conception of democracy are peculiar to conditions of his time. For example, there is his disposition to favor agriculture because it fostered qualities which qualified people to govern themselves: common sense, diligence, and self-reliance.

It was for the same reason that he promoted the right to acquire property in order to establish a sense of independence and responsibility.

But above all—and lastingly—he made education the key to every one of his proposals. Self-rule could not work if people were not somehow made good enough to govern. It was when the existing political arrangements should give assurance of sufficient "virtue and talent" in the citizen that we find the relevance of his much-quoted statement, "that government is best which governs least."

In Jefferson we find the underlying spirit of a government of free men under a Bill of Rights interpreted by an independent judiciary which, he said, "merits great confidence" because of the "learning and integrity" of the judges.

Under the Articles of Confederation, Jefferson had served as our envoy to France during the French Revolution, and he was immured in its ideals. Of course, one cannot state as a *fact* that human beings are born with certain rights. But to Jefferson these rights were, as he said, just common sense, and he stated these ideals as taken for granted. Today we are actually aware of how important such allegiance to human rights can be in generating a similar spirit throughout the world.

Jefferson was, in terms of our survey, a Lockean and not a Benthamite. None of the Founding Fathers was a Utilitarian. For lawyers practicing law, Austin's legal positivism usefully expresses the hard-boiled attitude of a lawyer dealing with cases arising out of the common law and legislation, especially criminal law. Austin's theory and Bentham's thought do not encompass the theory and spirit of our Bill of Rights. The Bill of Rights was not a part of the original Constitution framed by delegates numbering many lawyers. It was added only later when some states refused to sign the Constitution unless it was added. From France, Jefferson wrote to Madison that it should be added as a set of amendments to the Constitution and not be left to inference. It is embraced within the first ten amendments.

When we turn now to Holmes, I have concentrated on Holme's adoption of legal positivisim in his famous article "The Path of the Law," which also reflects a "pragmatic" twist deriving from his association with the early American pragmatists. A reader expecting me to present Holmes's eloquent and famous judicial opinions as a justice of the U.S. Supreme Court will be disappointed. At this point, I am compelled to bring the reader back to our track as we go on to consider, after Holmes, the influence of the thought of the pragmatic philosopher William James on Dean Roscoe Pound at Harvard, who gave a further American turn to legal philosophy with his writings on "sociological jurisprudence," followed by Karl Llewellyn who, inspired by Holmes and the pragmatic philosopher John Dewey, launched the movement of legal realism from Columbia.

The reader may still wonder why I have brought Jefferson in and have not kept a straight line from Austin to Holmes and the pragmatic development of legal positivism in America. I have included Jefferson at this point, not because he wrote on legal philosophy per se, but because I am making a transition to the American scene, and I believe it is important to note his influence in setting basic directions through is formulation of the Declaration of Independence which provided the philosophy of the Constitution.

6

Oliver Wendell Holmes, Jr. (1871–1947): The Pragmatic Turn

Introductory

Holmes is so preeminent and pivotal a figure in the development of legal thought in America that it would be futile to try to summarize the magnitude and depth of his revisionist books, articles, addresses, judicial opinions, and correspondences with Frederick Pollock, H. J. Laski, and Morris R. Cohen. Starting as a historian of law with his scholarly and comprehensive book *The Common Law,* he announced and demonstrated that the life of the law is experience and not simply a matter of logic.

For the line of development I am here tracing—from Bentham and Austin through Holmes to Legal Realism—I am urging your close attention to Holmes's famous article "The Path of the Law," written at the end of the nineteenth century, into which he crowded the contentions which changed the face of the law in America. Eloquently and brilliantly, he rephrased the legal positivist separation of law and morality while giving it a pragmatic, prospective, and human turn by focusing on the values of the judge in his decision making. He defined the law, not by its nature or structure or morality, but simply as a prediction of what a court will do. He writes law from the practical viewpoint of a lawyer trying to advise or defend a client. In thus expounding the common law, Holmes is well aware that his theory does not embrace that atypical side of the law known as "equity," nor does it deal with issues of Constitutional law, nor the meaning of law from some other broader or deeper perspective.

"The Path of the Law" is so important in our survey and covers so much ground in so concentrated a way that I have thought it necessary to present it as fully as possible while making my restatement of it easier to follow by breaking it up into sections and providing subheads. I invite the reader to a close study of this primary source.

Holmes tries to shock us into an acceptance of legal positivism by taking the attitude of a "bad man" who does not give a hoot-in-hell for any moral considerations, but just wants to know if he is going to have to go to jail or pay out some money for what he has done or plans to do. The pragmatic turn is his "prediction" theory and his exposure of the values implicit in judicial opinions.

The article appeared in a law review, and, since neither practicing lawyers nor nonlawyers are accustomed to read law reviews, I have taken special pains to take the reader by the hand as he studies this pregnant essay. Table 1 presents the rubrics I have used for each of the sections into which I have divided this article, and then I present the article divided into these sections and subsections according to this table of rubrics.

The article is based on an address delivered at the dedication of a new hall at the School of Law of Boston University in 1897. The address is intelligible to any intelligent reader and has enjoyed a wide readership among philosophers, political scientists, and the literate public. At the same time, it was meant to withstand professional scrutiny as a careful analysis of legal fundamentals. It was intended to influence the basic approach to law. It was published in the *Harvard Law Review*.

Holmes reveals that he is hewing a way through the jungles of jurisprudence by calling his essay, "The Path of the Law." In one sense, the title conveys a path with boundaries precisely delineated. In another sense, the title suggests an opening pathway for the future elaboration of legal thought. Both aspects, the limits of the law and the development of the law, are present in his essay. His influence has also extended in both directions: definitive Austinian demarcation and a pragmatic program of broader perspective. Since "The Path of the Law" epitomizes Holmes's view, I am making it the vehicle for the presentation of Holmes's views. Attacks upon

TABLE 1. "The Path of the Law"

I. *Introduction: Leading to the Two Underlying Principles of the Study of Law as a Profession*
The Study of Law as a Profession
Why the Profession of Law Exists
The Object of a Lawyer's Study: Prediction
The Materials of the Study
The Aim of Legal Thought (as Theory)
Why Past Prophecies Are Put into General Propositions
Rights and Duties as Prophecies
The Two Underlying Principles

II. *The Limits of the Law: Distinguishing Law from Morals*
The "Bad Man" Approach
The Distinction between Morals and Law
The Confusion in Our Conception of Law
The Confusion in Our Notion of Legal Duty
The Confusion as to Contractual Duty
The Confusion as to Malice
The Confusion in the Basis of Contract Law
The Overall Point: Avoiding Traps Set by Words of Moral Significance
The Limited Path of Law in Recapitulation

III. *The Development of Law: Beyond Logic*
The Forces Which Determine Its Context and Growth
The Basis of Tort Law
Weighing Social Advantages
The Ideal toward Which the Law Tends
History as a First Step toward Rational Revaluation
History Not to Be Overrated
Economics as a Step toward the Ideal of Studying Our Ends

IV. *Conclusion: The Role of Jurisprudence*
The Role of Jurisprudence in Clarifying the Ends of Law
Getting to the Bottom
Emphasis on Theory
Money and Imagination
Glimpse of the Infinite

Holmes have not always been predicated on careful consideration of the actual content of his essay and of its implications. By planting our feet firmly on "The Path of the Law," we shall traverse the essence of his thought. In summarizing and expounding the essay, I have taken the liberty of interpolating some interpretive comments to make it easier to follow his condensed analysis.

Introduction: Leading to the Two Underlying Principles of the Study of Law as a Profession

The Study of Law as a Profession

Jurisprudence may be approached from many different avenues. Holmes makes it very clear that he is discussing law as a subject of study—the study of law as a profession. A law school is erected for the purpose of training lawyers. How should law be studied by those who are to become lawyers? He opens incisively: "When we study law we are not studying a mystery but a well-known profession." The law may be a mystery. But the profession of law is not. If we study what the profession does, we may learn what the law is.

In the practice of the profession of law, as Holmes views it, the work of the law relates centrally to the courts. For a lawyer either appears before courts or advises people in such a way as to keep them out of courts. The two functions are recognized in the British distinction between the barrister, who does nothing but appear in courts, and the solicitor, who renders advice but never tries a case in court. Lawyers in America in Holmes's day were not as specialized as they are today, and indeed even today any lawyer might, in the course of a general practice, try a case. In America we allude to a lawyer as an "attorney" and "counsellor-at-law," observing thereby something of the same distinction England makes.

We know from Mark de Wolf Howe's biography of Holmes that his own brief experience at the bar began in the office of trial lawyers. Because he was also a judge, Holmes may have overemphasized the orientation of the legal profession to the trial of cases. Much of the work of lawyers today is not work in the courts, but office work; and much of the office work is not simply advice on how to keep out of court. It is work involved with strategies of corporate finance, with advice about ways of doing business or securing benefits, or it is other kinds of office work having no direct reference to the courts or any other tribunal. Quite a lot of the work of the lawyer today is likely to be directed, if to any tribunal, to some tribunal other than the courts: some administrative agency, either a local agency or a national one like the Securities and Exchange Commission (S.E.C.), or some arbitration board set up by the parties in lieu of a judge and a court trial. Even so, the ultimate reference is to the courts, because, in any final analysis, the legal papers which are drawn must be defensible in court, if attacked, and the determinations of other tribunals are subject to review in the courts. Much of law study, at any rate, is still today involved with the disputes which have given rise to litigation and have been disposed of by the courts. Whatever else a lawyer may learn or do, he must at least know how to analyze law cases which have been in the courts. Doctors bury their mistakes; judges publish theirs. The record is preserved in reports of cases published for lawyers' use. We call them "cases"; they are actually opinions of appellate courts, that is, courts of appeal, reviewing the work of the trial court, especially the trial court's charge to the jury. Appellate court opinions are still the main materials of law study, though such study has been broadened thanks to Holmes's influence. One sometimes wonders if the ready accessibility of judicial opinions in bound volumes or casebooks is not a principal factor in the persistence of their use as pedagogical tools, to the neglect of other phases of law work. But it is also true that the law considered as a body of intellectual rules, is manifested in these judicial opinions.

Why the Profession of Law Exists?

A recognized profession fulfills some social function. It renders a service which people need and for which they will pay. Why will people pay lawyers to argue cases before judges or give advice? The reason is, says Holmes, that, under certain circumstances, persons find themselves up against not only this or that person, but up against the mighty power of the state. The state has a legitimate monopoly of the public force. The weight of organized society is channeled through the courts in a vast array of situations, and our judges are entrusted with the command of this public force. If a person does not obey the court, even in a civil or noncriminal judgment where the dispute has been between two private parties, other officials, such as sheriffs and marshalls, will follow through the court's orders by going after him and seizing his property or putting him in jail. This public force is so overwhelming that no one can ignore it; and everyone necessarily must fear the prospect of encountering it. People need to know when—and to what extent—they will be running the risk of bucking up against something so strong, so much stronger than they are. To appraise this risk—the circumstances and degree—requires special knowledge. To find out when this danger is to be feared becomes a professional business. Thus lawyers are born.

The Object of a Lawyer's Study: Prediction

When we study law, therefore, as a professional discipline, we are really studying an art of prediction: "the prediction of the incidence of the public force through the instrumentality of the courts."

Will the ax fall? What will the penalties or the damages be? That is what the client wants to know. That is what the lawyer must learn how to tell. The reference is necessarily a future reference. That is why Holmes emphasizes that the referent is a prospective one—a prediction. (Holmes's view is sometimes called the "prediction theory of law.")

The Materials of the Study

In order to be able to make such predictions, a lawyer must be familiar with certain materials—the materials for the study of law. These materials are always increasing; they have been accumulating in this country and in England for some six hundred years: they are reports of cases which have been decided by the courts, they are legal treatises written by legal scholars, and they are the various statutes passed by the legislature. These cases, treatises, and statutes comprise the materials of the traditions of what we know as Anglo-American common law.

The Aim of Legal Thought (as Theory)

To Holmes, the meaning of every new effort of legal thought is (1) to make the "prophecies" of the past more precise, and (2) to generalize them into a system. The court precedents drawn from the past are really embalmed prophecies—live enough in their own day as reflections of what some lawyer had to predict to some worried client that a court would do.

Why Past Prophecies Are Put into General Propositions

The reason why the prophecies of the past are put into general propositions is simply to make them easier to be remembered and understood. The reason is purely one of convenience and mnemonics: to aid in studying them, in remembering them, and in understanding them. It is a practical reason only; there is nothing sacrosanct about these generalities. The prophecies of the past, thus generalized and systematized, tend to recur in each generation and to get restated for the current generation. Thus the earliest reports of cases are not too important, except historically.

Rights and Duties as Prophecies

When we have the past prophecies (the precedents) gathered in this way, we tend to think of the rights and duties of which they speak as though they were abstractions—as something apart from the consequences of their violation. We think of them as apart from, and independent of, the burdens or penalties imposed by the court for breach of duty or invasion of a right. We think of the "sanction" of the court as though it were something added—or added afterwards. We lose sight of the integral and inescapable meaning of a legal duty, however, if we think of it in this way—as something which can be differentiated, say, from the money we must pay if we breach it.

Holmes is very much concerned to make that point, in order, as he says, that we might not put the cart before the horse. Holmes wants to hammer in the realization that "a legal duty so-called is nothing but a prediction that if a man does or omits certain things he will be made to suffer in this or that way by judgment of the court."

Lawyers, wanting to be able to prophesy the actions of the courts, study these accumulated prophecies of the past for that reason. The old prophecies enable the lawyer in turn to make new and vital prophecies to serve the immediate purpose of his client. The old prophecies (the "precedents") are his instruments of prediction. It is this body of "systematized prediction" which, says Holmes, we have been accustomed to call the "law." In studying it, Holmes presents two "principles."

The Two Underlying Principles

The first of these is to keep law from getting confused with morals, to keep it within its own appropriate limits, on its own narrow path. The second of these is to recognize that though the form of legal reasoning is "logical," its ground is really legislative—a choice of values—and that this is the broad key to its development.

We may speak of these two principles as basic principles in two senses. (1) They are primary if we are to analyze and understand law correctly and clearly. (2) Both, if developed, would lead us into the realization of two *ideal* projections urged by Holmes: (1) the draining out of the law of all words of moral significance, and (2) the overt expression of legal decisions as estimates of competing social advantage. That is to say the explicit articulation of the grounds of decision, as contained in the judge's opinion, as being a balance of values or policies.

The Limits of the Law: Distinguishing Law from Morals

The "Bad Man" Approach

As we undertake to study the law, the first thing for us to be clear about is *the limits of our study.*

Initially we must therefore seek to dispel the confusion between morality and law. Otherwise we shall never see the law as law, in its own terms, unfudged by other guides to conduct—comprised in our notions of morality such as rules of ethics or even of etiquette—

which are not law because they are not enforced by courts. This confusion sometimes rises to conscious theory, but often it makes trouble without ever reaching the point of consciousness. Says Holmes:

> You can see very plainly that a bad man has as much reason as a good one for wishing to avoid an encounter with the public force, and therefore you can see the practical importance of the distinction between morality and law. A man who cares nothing for an ethical rule which is believed and practised by his neighbors is likely nevertheless to care a good deal to avoid being made to pay money, and will want to keep out of jail if he can.

Holmes is at pains to warn—a warning often overlooked by his critics—that the insistence on this "bad man" approach and this rigorous distinction between morality and law—made for the purpose of analytic clarity—is not to be misinterpreted as a total philosophy of cynicism. The law, he reminds us, is a witness and a repository of our moral life. "Its history is the history of the moral development of the race." The practice of law, despite crude jokes about lawyers, tends to make good citizens and good men. This is not the point. The point is to grasp clearly the difference between law and morals for one purpose only, for a single end: to learn and understand the law. (Remember that he is talking throughout about the study of law.) In order to accomplish this purpose, one must take hold of what specifically marks the law. To master its specific marks, the student of law should try, while studying the law, to imagine indifference to other and greater things. In some other and broader perspective, this distinction between law and morals may be of no importance. But for the study of law as a profession, it is of the first importance. We cannot criticize Holmes as being indifferent to morals because he insists on this Austinian distinction.

Thus, almost incidentally, we have been slipped into Holmes's "bad man" theory of the law. Perhaps there never was a man as bad as Holmes's straw man. But he needed the bad man as an electrifying symbol to wake us out of sloppy habits of legal analysis. How can legal analysis be clear and precise if we are never sure whether we are talking morals or law? Holmes thought there had been no appreciable philosophy of law prior to Austin, and he restates Austin in terms of a bad man as a rhetorical shocker.

It offends our sensibilities to be told to think of the law as something a bad man worries about. But it is when our sensibilities are shocked that we are most likely to start thinking. We are likely to be more impressed if we are told not only that the bad man thinks that way, but so also does Holmes—a former chief judge of the Supreme Judicial Court of Massachusetts, a former professor at Harvard Law School, an associate justice of the Supreme Court of the United States, and the distinguished scholar whose Lowell Lectures on "The Common Law" had already become a classic in the bold breadth of their painstaking historical research and the imagination which infused and integrated it.

The remainder of this first half of Holmes's address thus deals with the deleterious effects of confusing morals and law, the central importance of distinguishing them, and the helpfulness in doing so if we take the bad man as our guide. He may be a bad man, but he is a good guide, that is, if clarity in the study of law is what we are after.

The Distinction between Morals and Law

This distinction between morals and law, then, is of prime importance if we wish to study the law aright and to master it as a professional business. The limits of the law must be well and clearly understood. Its enclousre—as a body of past prophecy or dogma—must be seen to be within quite definitely drawn lines.

The practical reason for the distinction has been shown:

> If you want to know the law and nothing else, you must look at it as a bad man, who cares only for the material consequences which such knowledge enables him to predict, not as a good one, who finds his reasons for conduct, whether inside the law or outside of it, in the vaguer sanctions of conscience.

There is an equally strong theoretical reason for the distinction: it makes it possible to reason soundly on law. We ordinarily tend easily to slip from the domain of law to the domain of morals without perceiving it—and we are sure to do so if we do not keep the boundary in mind. The mere force of language leads us to do so, because the law is full of phraseology drawn from morals. The law talks about rights and duties, negligence and intent, malice, etc. Nothing is easier or more common in legal reasoning than to take these words in their moral sense and thus fall into fallacy.

Consider, for example, the "rights of man" spoken of in a *moral* sense. We mean *man's individual freedom* and the *limits of interference* with it—the limits of interference, that is, as prescribed by conscience or by some ideal (or standard or principle), however we may have reached it. Yet laws are enforced which pass this limit of interference, as many consciences would draw the limit, or as it may be drawn by the enlightened views of the time. Nothing but confusion of thought can possibly result from assuming that the rights of man, *in a moral sense,* therefore, are equally rights in the eyes of the law. No one would deny that we enforce through the courts statutes which many regard as wrong. Nor would we all agree on which statutes were wrong ones. But when the courts enforce such statutes, we do have "law."

We can, no doubt, think of some extreme statute which the legislature would not dare to enact—even if there were no Constitutional restrictions—because the community would rise in rebellion and fight. In that sense we may say law is limited by morality, if indeed the law is not actually a part of morality. But these limits are not coextensive with *any particular system of morals*. In such a case, a statute would be empty words simply because it could not be enforced, not because it was wrong. It has been said that the German population would rise if you raised the price of beer two cents.

The Confusion in Our Conception of Law

We have the fundamental question: What constitutes the law?

To Holmes the answer was quite clear: it is not something different from what is decided by the courts—by the courts of Massachusetts in Massachusetts, by the courts of England in England. It is not a deduction from principles of ethics. Nor is it a deduction from some admitted or give axioms, nor some system of reason, as some text writers say, nor something else which may or may not coincide with the decisions of the courts. Our friend, the bad man, we find, "does not care two straws for the axioms or deductions, but that he does want to know what the Massachusetts or English courts are likely to do in fact." Says Holmes: "I am much of his mind. The prophecies of what the courts will do in fact, and nothing more pretentious, are what I mean by the law."

We have seen that he has previously defined the law as the body of systematized predictions or "dogmas." But the difference in terms is only one of stance: looking *ahead*—as a lawyer does with a client and a case on his hands—a lawyer is trying to predict what a court will do. In order to make that prediction, he must look *back* upon the precedents or systematized predictions of the past (the "dogmas") to ascertain their likely effect upon his court. Both are embraced within Holmes's purview, but it is refreshing and realistic—an illustration of pragmatic prospectiveness—to place the stress on *predictability,* and to make quite distinct that the lawyer is predicting a judgment of his particular court, the only legal judgment which counts.

The Confusion in Our Notion of Legal Duty

Legal "duty" is the law's widest conception. The word is filled with contents drawn from morals. But what does it mean to our old friend, the bad man? "Mainly, and in the first place, a prophecy that if he does certain things he will be subjected to disagreeable consequences by way of imprisonment or compulsory payment of money."

Indeed, if the bad man has to pay a sum of money when he does a certain thing, it does not matter to him what it is called: whether it is called a "fine" or a "tax." Similarly, if the state takes a man's property (by "eminent domain" under the well-known Constitutional power to condemn private property for a public purpose) or some other private person takes it (by what the law calls "conversion") and cannot return it, what redress has he? In both cases—leaving the criminal law penalties aside—his redress is the same: the party taking his property (whether it is the state or the private converter) must pay its fair value—as determined by a jury. What is the significance, asks Holmes, of calling one taking of the property "right" and the other taking of the property "wrong"? We are giving the takings a moral characterization that has no legal effect. The practical consequence is that a compulsory payment must be made in either case—whether the act is praised or blamed, whether law allows it (as under eminent domain) or prohibits it (as a trespass). It makes no difference to the bad man whether he parks his car illegally and pays a fine, or whether he puts it in a garage and pays a fee.

Quite a few people are in that situation in our congested cities: only they don't usually think of themselves that way.

> You see how the vague circumference of the notion of duty shrinks and at the same time grows more precise when we wash it with cynical acid and expel everything except the object of our study, the operations of the law.

Ah, now, here we have it more precise still: the operations of the law, not the law as a handmaiden of morality, not the law as a mirror recording man's shifting relations to man, but the law only and simply in *its operations. That,* and that alone, is the object of our study, as Holmes conceives the study of law to be for someone who is preparing to be a lawyer. He must master the intricacies of the operations of law.

The Confusion as to Contractual Duty

The confusion between morals and law is most manifest in the law of contract. Duties under a contract are often invested with a kind of "mystic significance" beyond what can be fully explained. But the duty to keep a contract simply means a prediction that you must pay damages if you don't perform your undertaking. *Damages* is the law's word for the money, the compensatory sum, that must be payed to make up for failure to perform under the contract. That is all a contractual duty means. By the same token, leaving criminal penalties aside, a man must pay a compensatory sum if he wrongs someone with whom he has no contract—"commits" a "tort" (as we say in the law).

> If you commit a tort, you are liable to pay a compensatory sum. If you commit a contract, you are liable to pay a compensatory sum unless the promised event comes to pass, and that is all the difference.

Holmes finds the same manner of approach in the classic and traditional approach of Lord Coke himself; and he agrees with it:

"But such a mode of looking at the matter stinks in the nostrils of those who think it advantageous to get as much ethics into the law as they can."

Holmes recognizes this approach to be that of the "law" court as distinguished from an "equity" court, which will grant (take the exceptional step of granting) an injunction in advance of an act and punish disobedience. But for the purpose of his general theorizing, he suggests disregarding the atypical situation and focussing on the typical one. The typical and usual situation is the one, under our system, where one acts and then takes the consequences. A person suffers the consequences if the judge, like an umpire at a ball game, finds he has made an error.

I do not find it difficult to agree with Holmes that, for the purpose of trying to achieve theoretical clarity in a field where it is so hard, in view of all the complexity, to do so, we are justified in leaving so-called equity situations out of account, because it is the rare and unusual case which will, under exceptional circumstances, justify the intervention of a court to prevent someone in advance from doing something and punish him if he disobeys the mandate of the court. The equity side of the law came in historically through special appeals to the chancellor, who was a clergyman.

The Confusion as to Malice

The term *malice* has quite different meanings in morals and in law, and yet this difference has been obscured by giving the same label to two principles which have little to do with each other. In morals, says Holmes, the term connotes a malevolent motive. Originally it may have had such a moral connotation in the early development of our law. Thus when a man told a story about another which was false (that is, engaged in "slander"), the story teller was held liable for the injury inflicted by his slanderous statements if he told the story with a malevolent motive—with what we commonly call "malice." He was not held legally responsible, if he told the story innocently, without any such bad motive. Today lawyers still charge that the statements were made maliciously when, as lawyers, they undertake to state a case, but they do not mean to say anything about motives; all they mean today is that the tendency of the conduct of the slanderer was to cause the harm.

The Confusion in the Basis of Contract Law

Here, in the course of continuing and deepening his analysis of the law of contract, Holmes gets down to telling us more specifically what he means by morals: "Morals," he says, "deals with the actual *internal* state of the individual's mind, what he *actually* intends," (Italics added.)

It will at once appear to the perceptive reader that Holmes, at this point, is in the process of making a slip over to a different meaning for morals than the one he has previously employed. He has heretofore been using the term *morals* to mean something more, by way of a sanction for one's conduct, than the mere naked pressure derived from a fear of what coercions will be imposed by a court. The bad man is interested in those coercions and those coercions only. But the non–bad man is interested also in morals: he cares about such factors as an "ethical" precept which is believed in and practised by his neighbors, or as the "vague" promptings or dictates of conscience. *That* is the distinction Holmes has been making up to this point. But, beginning with his discussion of malice, and continuing now with his discussion of the basis of contract law, he slides into a different point. Now he is talking, not about moral rules contrasted with legal rules as sanctions or determinants of one's conduct; now he is talking about the inner state of an individuals mind, as contrasted with his external actions (irrespective of the inner state of his mind). Holmes is now about to intensify a discussion—already started in his analysis of malice—of the so-called external standard (or criterion) as a basis for one's being held liable by a court in a lawsuit. Whether or not a court should use an external touchstone, viewing an individual's actions *only,* or another touchstone; namely, the inner state of his mind when he acted: that is the point Holmes is now involved in discussing. It is really quite a different point from the one he started discussing; namely, the confusion between law, as a coercion imposed by a court, and morality as a differentiable determinant of conduct.

Let us go on, following him in his analysis of the external standard, however, to see where his present discussion is leading.

Holmes is firmly set against any intrusion into the law of contracts of "morals" in the sense in which he is *now* using the term:

the actual internal state of the individual's mind, what he *actually* intends, if one gets inside of his head somehow. Holmes would like to eliminate that kind of moral factor from the law of contracts because of the confusion it brings about there. Traditionally, the language of the law, in dealing with contracts, is language which smacks of morals in that sense, and hence confuses our thought when we try to see clearly what it is we mean. Traditionally a contract is talked about as a "meeting of the minds of the parties." Thus there would be no contract, if their "minds" had not "met"; that is to say, if one party, for example, *intended* one thing and the other party intended something else. But in the law of contracts, nothing is more certain than that parties may be bound by a contract to do things which neither of them intended. Suppose a contract is made which binds a party to do something—but no time is mentioned. One party thinks it means at once, in a week, say. The other party thinks it means whenever he is ready. The court decides that it means within a reasonable time. The parties are bound by the contract not as either one of them intended or understood or interpreted it, but as the court interpreted it. Neither of them meant what the court determines they meant by what they said.

"In my opinion," says Holmes,

> no one will understand the true theory of contract or be able even to discuss some fundamental questions intelligently until he has understood that all contracts are formal, that the making of a contract depends not on the agreement of two minds in one intention, but on the agreement of two sets of external signs—not on the parties having *meant* the same things but on their having *said* the same thing.

The Overall Point: Avoiding Traps Set by Words of Morals Significance

In giving two meanings of the word *morals,* Holmes makes two distinct points.

First, that law as a prediction of what a court will do by way of imposing coercions (in the form of fines, damages, or imprisonment) is not to be confounded with other sanctions of conduct, such as conscience or ideals or our neighbor's opinion.

Second, that law, as in contract law, is concerned with an external standard—the conduct of the parties (or their formal signs)—not with morals in the sense of the inner intent of their minds.

These might well appear to be two quite different points. But there is an overall sense in which both these points serve to make Holmes's major point. His underlying point is that "words of moral significance," with which legal analysis and discussion are replete, lay traps for us, both in legal practice and theoretical speculation. They muddle lawyers as they try to focus on the true cynosure of their concern: a prediction of what a court's coercions will be. They muddle us, too, if we are laymen, for laymen also are often mixed up as to where law ends and morality begins, or how they are (or are not) interfused and related. More specifically in the branch of the law known as contract law, we get into trouble if we try to probe into morals, in Holmes's second sense: people's intents in the inside of their minds. We will do better by just looking at external acts (was the action likely to result in harm?) and signs (what are the words of the contract which the parties signed?).

Holmes warns us that he is not trying to work out a theory in detail. He is throwing out some hints. He is trying, by doing so, to throw some light on the "narrow path of legal doctrine" and on two pitfalls which lie close to this narrow path—and into which the unwary will easily fall.

The Limited Path of Law in Recapitulation

The narrow path of legal doctrine—what is it now in recapitulation? It is to view the law as a prediction of the coercions a court will actually impose. It is to view the traditional doctrines of the law as a body of "dogma" consisting of systematized past predictions (known more familiarly as precedents), which the lawyer, by mastering them, can use as a tool for the prediction he is presently called upon to make in the given case. It is a path which can be sharply distinguished from the moral thickets and underbrush which surround and flank it. If we do not observe its narrow limits, we shall slip and fall into quagmires and gullies by the wayside. We shall talk of ethical rules and voices of conscience; we shall talk of the inner content of our minds and of our intent, when we should keep our eye on court coercions to be anticipated and on external acts and signs.

The traps which are laid on either side of the narrow path are traps of language, of legal language, which leads us astray. Holmes is sounding a semantic warning. Be on guard against the overtones of the words which are current in the law: they are words heavy with moral overtones and associations; and they will obscure your path. Words are merely the counters of wise men, he might have quoted from one of his masters, Hobbes; they are the coin only of fools.

He now concludes this first half of his address, devoted to the first of the initials he fears; Viz, the failure to recognize the limits of the narrow path of the law and the tendency to confuse it with the broad highways of morality.

"For my own part," he says,

> I often doubt whether it would not be a gain if every word of moral significance could be banished from the law altogether, and other words adopted which should convey legal ideas unclothed by anything outside the law. We should lose the fossil records of a good deal of history and the majesty got from ethical associations, but by ridding ourselves of an unnecessary confusion we should gain very much in the clearness of our thought.

Clarity of thought: that was Holmes's sovereign consideration in laying out the path of the law with such precision in its naked contours.

So much for the limits of the law; so much for the first of the basic "principles" to be observed in the study of law as a profession; so much for the fence we must build around the law qua law to keep from straying off the narrow path.

It is highly doubtful that we shall ever substitute neutral symbols for the highly charged terms which we have been accustomed to use in the law. But that we should be alerted to separate the moral meanings of these words from their legal meanings—and the domain of morals from the domain of law—these hygienes of the mind Holmes's analysis brings. It does not, of course, follow that law has nothing to do with morals. But a lawyer can keep his analysis straight if he does not fuse the two and faces directly problems of the relation of one to the other. A man who consults a lawyer is looking for a different kind of guidance than a man who consults his preacher. If the client wants his lawyer's ethical judgment also, he will get it more clearly if the lawyer distinguishes clearly between the ethical opinion and the legal opinion.

The Development of Law: Beyond Logic

We now turn to the second principle in the study of law: the recognition that the key to the development of law is legislative (not logic alone). Holmes is fighting the inherited tradition which thinks of law as simply a matter of logical deductions from given legal rules. The law, he says, has developed "legislatively," that is to say, by a choice among competing values or policies.

The Forces Which Determine Its Content and Growth

What are the forces at work in the development of law? What principles explain its growth?

It is here that we run into the second fallacy Holmes wants to expose. This fallacy is the notion that the only force at work in the development of the law is logic.

As in the case of "morals" or of "law" itself, we must be careful to indicate what Holmes means when he speaks of "logic." What he is warning against is the notion that any legal system can be developed, like mathematics, from some general axioms of conduct. It is logic in this sense that he wants to dismiss as the governing principle of legal development. Any one who looks at a legal textbook might fall into the pitfall of thinking that law is just a working out of certain axioms, as Euclid developed a system of geometry from certain axioms.

This is the "natural error of the schools," says Holmes, as if to suggest that one would expect some academician, some professor of law, working with ideas in the privacy of his study, to fall into the error of thinking that law is a logical system which has developed from a few initial self-evident or inherited axioms; and that what has been so developed *is* indeed the law. *That* is law; and there is naught else which is law! Holmes reports the remark of an eminent judge who had been heard to say: he never let a decision go until he was absolutely sure it was right! As if there ever could be such a thing! And, from this standpoint, dissenting judges are reproached, as if they were not doing their sums correctly (or so the dissenters might blame the majority!), and as if to imply that, if they would just take a little more trouble and time, logical agreement would inevitably ensue.

That is a "natural" way for lawyers to think. Lawyers have been trained to processes of logic: of deduction and analogy and fine discrimination verbally. They are most at home with these processes. Judicial decisions are cast mainly in the language of logic. This working with a logical method and form appeals to men's longing for "certainty" and for "repose." But "certainty generally is illusion, and repose is not the destiny of man." Any conclusion can be given a logical form. But what lies behind the logical form?

> Behind the logical form lies a judgment as to the relative worth and importance of competing legislative grounds, often an inarticulate and unconscious judgment it is true, and yet the very root and nerve of the whole proceeding.

A judge can always say that some contractual condition must be met because he finds it "implied" in the contract as he interprets it. But why does he find it implied?

> It is because of some belief as to the practice of the community or of a class or because of some opinion as to policy.

It is because of some attitude about which we cannot be exact. There is a battleground where a decision can embody the preference of a given court at a given time and place. A large part of the law is always open to reconsideration upon some change, even a slight change, in the "habit of the public mind."

A single example illustrates how we choose between competing values, scarcely realizing we are doing it sometimes, when the preference has become routine: "Why is a man at liberty to set up a business which he knows will ruin his neighbor? It is because the public good is supposed to be best subserved by free competition." Such judgments of relative importance may vary in different times and places. Today, almost a century after Holmes's address, certain types of competition are deemed "unlawful competition."

Since it is the "public mind" which is involved, sometimes the issue is determined by that segment of the public mind which comprises a jury. The following example, which Holmes gives, is characteristically candid.

Why does a judge instruct a jury that an employer is not liable to an employee for an injury received in the course of his employment unless the employer is negligent, and why does the jury generally find for the plaintiff if the case is allowed to go to them? (Holmes's implication is, of course, that the jury finds for the plaintiff-employee even if the defendant-employer has not been negligent.) It is because the *traditional* policy of our law is to confine liability to cases where a prudent man might have foreseen the danger, while the *inclination of a very large part of the community* is to make certain classes of persons *insure* the safety of those with whom they deal.

The reference to "insure" is doubtless a reference to the proposal—then only a proposal—for workmen's compensation insurance, now a fixture of our legal scene.

"There is a concealed, half-conscious battle on the question of legislative policy, and if any one thinks that it can be settled deductively, or once for all," he is wrong as a matter of theory and of acceptable practice.

Holmes then proceeds to open up for possible reconsideration—without being prepared to say how he would resolve it—the basic theory of our inherited tort law. He points out that it came from the old days of occasional isolated wrongs (such as an assault or a slander, where the damages lie where they fall on the individual and isolated defendant). But the torts which busy our courts today are mainly torts which are incidental to some familiar business of today: a factory or a railroad. The business considers that it will have such liabilities, estimates the cost, and passes it on in the price charged to the public which pays it. (Though he does not say so, the price includes the cost of the premium for the insurance taken out against these risks.) "The public really pays the damage, and the question of liability, if pressed far enough, is really the question how far it is desirable that the public should insure the safety of those whose work it uses." He points out, realistically, that in such cases the jury usually finds for the plaintiff. And he sums it all up in the two sentences which have become famous through frequent quotation:

> I think that the judges themselves have failed adequately to recognize their duty of weighing considerations of social advantage. The duty is inevitable, and the result of the often proclaimed judicial aversion to deal with such considerations is simply to leave the very ground and foundation of judgments inarticulate and often unconscious, as I have said.

Weighing Social Advantages

Since lawyers were not traditionally taught to think in these terms (and I may add that today they are still not taught to do so sufficiently), they often, scarcely realizing it, give expression (when they are judges) to economic (or other) doctrines which may no longer be pertinent. And thus Holmes concludes:

> I cannot but believe that if the training of lawyers led them habitually to consider more definitely and explicitly the social advantage on which the rule they lay down must be justified, they sometimes would hesitate where now they are confident, and see that really they were taking sides upon debatable and often burning questions.

So much for the "fallacy of logical form"; so much for the supposition that only logic is at work in the development of law; so much for the need more candidly to estimate and state the underlying social factors which enter into a judgment of the court and the development of the law through the courts.

The Ideal toward Which the Law Tends

Holmes then projects a remote ideal—an ideal not in the sense of a desired and imminently achievable end (such as John Dewey calls a pragmatic end-in-view), but an ideal in the sense of a distant star beckoning us to fairer horizons. "We still are far from the point of view which I desire to see reached." Holmes tells us: "No one has reached it or can reach it yet."

He regards us, as of the time when he was speaking, the tail end of the nineteenth century, as *at the beginning of what he called a "philosophic reaction."* (He is doubtless thinking of Utilitarianism and pragmatism.) He described it as "a re-consideration of the worth of doctrines which for the most part still are taken for granted without any deliberate, conscious, and systematic questioning of their grounds." The re-consideration of which he speaks is the realist outcome of Anglo-American philosophy of law in the Legal Realist movement which Holmes inspired.

Then follows a remarkably sympathetic and pithy description of the almost imperceptible way in which our law naturally develops even when unpricked by the spur of rational criticism deliberately prodding its advance.

> The development of our law has gone on for nearly a thousand years, like the development of a plant, each generation taking the inevitable next step, mind, like matter, simply obeying a law of spontaneous growth. It is perfectly natural and right that it should be so. Imitation is a necessity of human nature. . . . Most of the things we do, we do for no better reason than that our fathers had done them or that our neighbors do them, and the same is true of a larger part than we suspect of what we think. The reason is a good one, because our short life gives us no time for a better, but it is not the best.

And then the great challenge:

> It does not follow, because we all are compelled to take on faith at second hand most of the rules on which we base our action and our thought, that each of us may not try to set some corner of his world in the order of reason, or that all of us collectively should not aspire to carry reason as far as it will go throughout the whole domain.

It is not necessary that we should claim to know what is permanently best for men or what is absolutely best for the cosmos. Nor do we need to affirm universal validity for our social ideals or for the principles which we think should be embodied in law or legislation. We may be content if we can prove what is best for here and now. In these remarks, Holmes sets himself apart from the natural law theorists who, he says in another essay, simply had a craving for the superlative.

What remains basically true is "that a body of law is more rational and civilized when every rule it contains is referred articulately and definitely to an end which it subserves, and when the grounds for desiring that end are stated or are ready to be stated in words."

What is the conventional and usual practice?

> At present, in very many cases, if we want to know why a rule of law has taken its particular shape, and more or less if we want to know why it exists at all, we go to tradition.

Somewhere in the past, in the needs of Norman kings or beyond, in the assumptions of some then-dominant class, without any generalized ideas, "we find out the practical motive for what now is best justified by the mere fact of its acceptance and that men are accustomed to it."

History as a First Step toward Rational Revaluation

Thus when we have sought to study law rationally today, our study is to a large extent the study of history; and history must always be part of our rational study. It is the *first step* (but the first step only) toward what Holmes calls "enlightened scepticism," which is the deliberate reconsideration of the worth of our rules.

"When you get the dragon out of his cave on to the plain and in the daylight, you can count his teeth and claws, and see just what is his strength. But to get him out is only the first step. The next is either to kill him, or to tame him and make him a useful animal."

Thus for the rational study of law we shall need more than the "black-letter man" of the present, the expert in the logical analysis of boldface legal rules found in digests and textbooks. The "man of the future is the man of statistics and the master of economics." He is perhaps thinking of someone like the distinguished Boston lawyer Louis Brandeis, who became his colleague and frequent companion in dissent on the U.S. Supreme Court.

Then another celebrated passage:

> It is revolting to have no better reason for a rule of law than that so it was laid down in the time of Henry IV. It is still more revolting if the grounds upon which it was laid down have vanished long since, and the rule simply persists from blind imitation of the past.

Even more fundamental questions still await a better answer than that we do as our fathers have done.

What have we, more than a blind guess, to show that the criminal law in its present form does not do more harm than good? Does punishment deter? Do we deal with criminals on proper principles? There is "weighty authority," says Holmes, in the only passage he quotes from another source, for the belief that the criterion of social reaction to the criminal should be the dangerousness of the criminal, not the nature of the crime. The authority he cites is Havelock Ellis.

History Not to Be Overrated

"Law is the business to which my life is devoted," he avows, "and I should show less than devotion if I did not do what in me lies to improve it, and, when I perceive what seems to me the ideal of its future, if I hesitated to point it out, to press toward it with all my heart." Having paid his tribute to history, he then puts it in perspective.

Since the basis of legal principle everywhere is tradition, we are ever in danger of making the role of history more important than it is. We must beware of antiquarianism, and we must remember that for our purposes our only interest in the past is for the light it throws upon the present.

> I look forward to a time when the part played by history in the explanation of dogma shall be very small, and instead of ingenious research we shall spend our energy on a study of the ends sought to be attained and the reasons for desiring them.

Economics as a Step toward the Ideal of Studying Our Ends

Deprecating the divorce between the schools of political economy and law, he suggests that every lawyer ought to seek an understanding of economics. In political economy we are called upon to consider the ends of legislation, and the means and costs of attaining them. "We learn that for everything we have to give up something else, and we are taught to set the advantage we gain against the other advantage we lose, and to know what we are doing when we elect."

Conclusion: The Role of Jurisprudence

The Role of Jurisprudence in Clarifying the Ends of Law

By *jurisprudence* Holmes means simply law in its most generalized form. In a sense, to seek a general rule in any ordinary law case is an effort of jurisprudence, although the English word *jurisprudence* is used for the most fundamental conceptions and the broadest rules. "One mark of a great lawyer is that he sees the application of the broadest rules." If a man goes into law and wants to be a master of it, he must look through the "incidents" and discern the "true basis" for prophecy. The highest courts sometimes flounder because they have no clear and accurate idea of what is meant by law or right or duty, and the like. It is a practical advantage to master Austin and his predecessors, Hobbes and Bentham, and his successors.

Getting to the Bottom

Holmes does not value the study of Roman law, for he thought it was better to master our own law, the Anglo-American common law, to its very bottom, than to master the difficult set of technicalities in another system of law.

How do you get to the bottom of our subject and command a liberal view of it?

> The means of doing that are, in the first place, to follow the existing body of dogma into its highest generalizations by the help of jurisprudence; next, to discover from history how it has come to be what it is; and, finally, so far as you can, to consider the ends which the several rules seek to accomplish, the reasons why those ends are desired, what is given up to gain them, and whether they are worth the price.

Emphasis on Theory

"We have too little theory in the law rather than too much, especially on this final branch of study."

Though his subject has been the study of law, Holmes remarks that he has said little about what is usual in that connection: the case system, textbooks, and other machinery with which the student comes in contact.

He is not interested in the mode of teaching, or whether it is from textbooks or casebooks, since ability and industry will master the material with any mode of teaching. Theory is his subject, not practical details.

> Theory is the most important part of the dogma of the law, as the architect is the most important man who takes part in the building of a house. The most important improvements of the last twenty-five years are improvements in theory. It is not to be feared as impractical, for, to the competent, it simply means going to the bottom of the subject. For the incompetent, it sometimes is true, as has been said, that an interest in general ideas means an absence of particular knowledge. . . . But the weak and foolish must be left to their folly. The danger is that the able and practical minded should look with indifference or distrust upon ideas the connection of which with their business is remote.

Money and Imagination

A man once hired a valet with the understanding that any faults were to result in deductions from his wages. One of his deductions was for lack of imagination. "The lack is not confined to valets," Holmes adds acidly.

The object of ambition, which is power, is generally present nowadays, says Holmes, in the form of money alone. Money is its most immediate form; and money is a proper object of desire. "The fortune is a measure of intelligence" is a good text to waken people out of a fool's paradise. But in the end, as Hegel says, it is the opinion, not the appetite, which has to be satisfied.

> To an imagination of any scope the most far-reaching form of power is not money; it is the command of ideas. The practical force controlling the conduct of men and governing the world today is to be found in Descartes or Kant, rather than Bonaparte.

> We cannot all be Descartes or Kant, but we all want happiness. And happiness, I am sure from having known many successful men, cannot be won simply by being counsel for great corporations and having an income of fifty thousand dollars. An intellect great enough to win the prize needs other food besides success.

Glimpse of the Infinite

He concludes with an unexpected metaphysical paean.

The remoter and more general aspects of the law are those which give it universal interest. It is through them that you not only become a great master in your calling, but connect your subject with the universe "and catch an echo of the infinite, a glimpse of its unfathomable process, a hint of the universal laws."

* * *

I am presenting Holmes and the subsequent American figures each in a separate chapter, each to be considered on his own terms. In the concluding chapter, after the reader has been able to form his own conclusions, I do some stitching together. Meanwhile, let us bear in mind that, as Holmes says, there are many avenues.

7

Roscoe Pound (1870–1964): Sociological Jurisprudence

William James, cofounder of the American philosophy of pragmatism, sought to put to rest traditional theories of ethics with his claim that the "essence of good is simply to satisfy demand." All demands cannot be satisfied conjointly, and so the guiding principle for ethics is "simply to satisfy at all times as many demands as we can." The echoes of Utilitarianism are clear enough.

Social Engineering

Roscoe Pound, the founder of American "sociological jurisprudence," was a Harvard colleague of James and served as dean of the Harvard Law School. That he was greatly influenced by James in basic approach comes out clearly in a much-quoted paragraph from his *Introduction to the Philosophy of Law*. "For the purpose of understanding the law today," he writes, "I am content with a picture of satisfying as much of the whole body of human wants as we may with the least sacrifice." He uses interchangeably the words *demands, wants, interests, expectations,* and *claims*. Certain claims are involved in the very existence of civilized society. The law must satisfy these expectations by giving effect to as much as it feasibly can. The law does so by an ordering of human conduct through the state. The law is engaged in "social engineering." (When I took John Dewey's course in "experimental logic" at Columbia he was fond of using the engineer as a prime example of "man thinking.") The result of Pound's voluminous writings was to shift attention from abstract legal terms like rights and duties to the social pressures which the law meets as it tries to effectuate various social interests. He is not interested in "law on paper"; he is interested in "law in action."

Once having embarked on this course, he proceeded to draw up an extensive catalogue of the interests which the law protects. In his earlier career, before studying law, Pound had been a botanist. The botanist is involved in the early stages of science which we call taxonomy, and, in a similar way, Pound proceeded to classify various interests, just as the botanist classifies plants. Felix Frankfurter tells us in his *Memoirs* that he and Pound were brought to the Harvard Law School at the same time to bring social referents to bear on the law. While Frankfurter went in the direction of relating law to politics and governmental administration, Pound went in the direction of working out a fresh approach to jurisprudence, drawing not only upon the English sources, but broad study of French and German jurists.

Individual and Social Interests

Pound proceeded to break down the various interests of the individual and the various interests of society, to the extent they can be separately viewed. He realized, of course, that there is an overlap and that the same interest can be viewed from either angle. The individual, for example, has an interest in his family; society also has an interest in the stability of the family, one of its major institutions.

Every business has to take inventory, and Pound may be said to have done it for the business of law. It may be a dull task, but it keeps us to see what societal interests we are dealing with and where we are in a certain time.

The individual is concerned with (1) his own well-being, (2) the well-being of his family, and (3) his economic security. Pound calls them interests of (1) personality, (2) domestic relations, and (3) material substance. "Personality" pertains to health, reputation, privacy, and freedom of expression. "Domestic relations" pertains to marriage and the relations of the members of the family to one another. "Material substance" pertains to property and contract rights.

Society demands (1) its own security and defense, (2) the wholesomeness of its environment (as by clean air), (3) prosperity (in the sense of a flourishing economy), (4) a sound legal system, and (5) certain values associated with the mind, morals, and religion.

In regrouping these social interests, he gives them the following formulation:

1. *general security:* peaceful order, safety, and health; the security of business dealings
2. *the security of social institutions:* not only the security of the state itself, but of marriage and freedom of speech
3. *general morals:* condemnation of dishonesty and corruption
4. *conservation:* maintenance of social resources we use in common
5. *general progress:* development in the satisfaction of our wants; improved legal institutions
6. *the life of each person:* living out his life

These are the wants of civilized society. They are very generally put. The lawyer will readily recognize actual branches of the law dealing with each of them: for example, acquisitions are dealt with by property law, transactions by contract law, peaceful order by criminal law, civil liberties by Constitutional law. It is not a static classification, for the social interest in "general progress" opens a door for newly emerging desires, leaving room for fresh claims and enhanced social engineering. After the New Deal, Pound added job security and workmen's compensation. A pragmatist is always prepared to make changes to cope with changing situations.

Though Pound also speaks of certain "public" interests, besides "social" interests, he seems to mean no more than the public interest in harmonizing the congeries of other interests.

Law as a Means to a Social End

To Pound, as Bentham, did not consider the law an end in itself, but a means to an end. An engineer in building bridges, not for the sake of the bridges per se, but in order to get us over the river.

Pound's reorientation was appreciated not only by pragmatic

philosophers, but by a rationalist philosopher like Morris R. Cohen and an idealist philosopher like William Hocking. His influence on jurisprudence was considerable, notably upon theorists like Julius Stone and George W. Paton in Australia and Edwin Patterson at Columbia Law School. The "legal realists" at Columbia liked to distinguish themselves from Pound, but I always felt they did not give him enough credit.

Pound's inventory is a comprehensive perspective on the basic concerns of our society. They are not often articulated in this explicit way. He enables us to become more aware of their pressure and their interrelation. As we consider how these interests are relatively weighted, we are made to realize that there are always shifting conflicts of value. Pound earmarks the interest in individual life as the most important interest.

Considering the wealth of books and articles bequeathed to us by Pound in his long life, it is, of course, inadequate to capsulate his contribution in this fashion. The interested reader may refer to his multivolume panorama entitled simply *Jurisprudence*. There are also cogent criticisms by legal realists like Jerome Frank, the lawyer and judge, and legal analysts like the philosopher, Herbert Morris. Contemporaries of Pound, like Morris R. Cohen and Felix S. Cohen, his philosopher-lawyer son, pioneering in developing American legal philosophy as a branch of philosophy, expressed profound gratitude to Pound for bringing philosophic perspective and depth to an exposition of law. They built upon his contribution, as did both Llewellyn and Cardozo and the legal realists whom we are next to consider.

8

John Dewey (1859–1953): The Activities of Law

John Dewey is not primarily a legal philosopher, but he must be included in this recital because his pragmatic departure from traditional philosophy was a seminal influence on Karl Llewellyn and the Legal Realist movement, which I shall discuss in the next chapter and which is the realist outcome of this book. Dewey and Holmes greatly admired each other, and together they represent a peak in American culture in its revolt against an American culture in its revolt against formalism in the early twentieth century. The pragmatist looks beyond verbal differences to their meaning in practical consequences in order to avoid purely verbal disputes. If the meaning of some term or proposition is disputed, the pragmatist asks if the practical consequences would require a different way of acting. If not, it is not a real difference, but only a formal or formulated difference.

Dewey explores the social implications. In the course of our experience, we come up against a problem. We must then engage in thinking—reflection—inquiry to solve the problem. Traditional formal logic will not help, because it is merely a logic of arrangement or exposition of what is already known. It supplies forms, like the syllogism, which are outside the subject matter of the problem. Dewey's logic of inquiry, on the other hand, is a logic of reconstruction, of planning an action.

When applied to law, Dewey's approach looks at legal rules to ascertain what they amount to in the activities they involve. Thus, besides legal rules, what Holmes called the "black-letter law" and Pound called the "law-in-books," Dewey would extend our understanding of the law by considering the activities involved: what courts *do,* what legislatures *do,* what administrative agencies *do.* Dewey, like Holmes and Bentham, leaves behind the theory of natural law. He looks at what is actually being done in our society by the institutions of the law. The word *law* for Dewey is a shorthand word for the rules of law *and* the activities of courts, legislatures, and governmental agencies.

Since Dewey does not emerge from the legal profession like Holmes, Pound, Llewellyn, and Cardozo, I shall not linger on his few articles on law, and I shall add only that Holmes praised Dewey's last book, *Experience and Nature;* that Cardozo thought Dewey had learned more about law than the lawyers had learned about philosophy; that Jerome Frank, an experienced trial lawyer, thought Dewey's description of what a trial lawyer does was the best account he had ever read; that Dewey taught a seminar in legal philosophy at the Columbia Law School; and that Llewellyn, in launching the Legal Realist movement, conceived himself to be doing for law what Dewey was doing for philosophy.

But Llewellyn was not really interested in Dewey's theory of logic, nor was he a Deweyan in every sense of Dewey's philosophy. Llewellyn shied away from "philosophy." What impressed him about Dewey was the way he gave a "fresh" look at what was going on and re-posed issues. Llewellyn confessed privately that he wanted to do for law what Dewey had done for art, politics, and education, but which he never did for law because, Llewellyn thought, Professor Patterson (with whom Dewey gave his seminar at the law school) led him into theories of logic instead of fresh reappraisal.

Dewey pointed out that previous philosophic discussions of law arose from the need to have principles to criticize (or justify) the extant legal rules and practices. Dewey said this need was exemplified historically in the central distinction between "positive law," the law as it actually exists, and "natural law" (the law of nature), which served as a standard or ideal or "ought" to which the positive law was supposed to conform. This distinction, Dewey observed, is no longer in vogue today except among those who may still follow the older natural law tradition which lasted intact through the seventeenth century.

But it nonetheless remains true that we do still have to distinguish between the extant law and the law as it should (or might) be. When Dewey speaks of the extant law he means to embrace all existing legal affairs, which include not only rules of law but legislative, judicial, and administrative practices. How can these legal affairs be suitably evaluated? What ground do we now have, and how can we organize it?

If we look only at the logical structure of a legal philosophy, that is to say exclusively at its intellectual basis, we are faced with a hopeless conflict. We avoid such frustration only when we realize that each of the varying legal philosophies is really telling us what *should be done* about the *practical problems* facing the philosopher *in his time and place:* what should be done and how to do it. There is no such thing as a universal or permanent or perennial philosophy of law.

Law cannot be viewed in isolation from our other social activities. It is part of a general social process at the same time that it intervenes in this process. It is itself a *process*. What does the law *do* in the social complex in which it arises? It is all right to use the term *law*, Dewey says, as long as we understand that the word is used to refer to this whole range of processes, saving us the trouble to specify every time that we are referring to legal rules *and* to the activities and decisions of judges, administrative agencies, and legislative bodies.

We can only tell what law is by seeing how it operates—what its effects or consequences are in the social milieu.

The move to *consequences* had already been made by Bentham. But previous empirical philosophers did not take cognizance of the function of human habits and social customs as Dewey does. Their relative slowness of change in earlier times led philosophers to think of them as permanent and static. Earlier philosophers did not realize that society is in constant flux. This is all we need to recognize why philosophers in earlier periods and cultural climates were disposed to set up some source *external* to society which they did not perceive as ongoing social activity. They spoke of God or God's reason or the "law of nature" (or even, to glance at French thought, which we are not including in our survey of the Anglo-

American tradition, the "general will" of Rousseau). Traditionally, philosophers have argued that in order to have value-standards by which to judge existing values, it is necessary to go outside of our ordinary experience.

But what Dewey stresses is that what we call the facts of society (the social facts) are really continuing activities. They are *ongoing*. If they were not ongoing, but were closed and completed, we could posit a standard for evaluating them which is outside of them, outside our actual experience. But we experience social facts as ongoing. Since they are ongoing they have consequences. If we want to change them or maintain them, we can find a group for doing so only by considering the consequences of these ongoing activities.

Let us acknowledge in a newly systematic way, Dewey urges, that social facts are ongoing and that all legal affairs occur within our ongoing concerns.

As we pursue this lead, Dewey adds in his role as educator, we will add not only to our understanding of the law, but also of the *never-ending* process of improving our standards of judgment, which, like the law's rules and activities, are *not fixed*.

Of Dewey's articles on law, the one most pertinent to our discussion sets out explicitly what he regards as a properly reasoned judicial decision. Its similarities to Holmes's observations in "The Path of the Law" are manifest. Such a decision must weigh the social consequences of a rule, and not merely its doctrinal antecedents. When weighing competing alternatives, a judge must choose the one that in the last analysis leads into the "social welfare." This way of putting it doubtless influenced Judge Cardozo, as we shall see when we examine his view in a later chapter. While the principles in the precedents in past decisions have been found useful in the past and are not to be ignored, they should be viewed as "working hypothesis" (as Cardozo also says) which are always open to reexamination to see what the results have been and how the working hypothesis would function in our society. Such judiciary thinking, in the last analysis choosing among competitive values by considering their practical consequences, is the only way, says Dewey, to assure that social advance through law will be intelligent and have a secure basis.

The reader will recall that Holmes had already made the point that judges inevitably weigh "considerations of social advantage," but that they are often unaware that they are doing so or are unable or unwilling to acknowledge that they are doing so because the formal conventions of judicial opinion writing are in the language of formal logic. The result, Holmes said, is "simply to leave the very ground and foundation of judgments inarticulate and often unconscious."

When Holmes speaks of the social ends which the law serves, he does not make it as clear as Dewey does that the social ends are not broad and general abstractions in the sky, but are what Dewey calls "ends-in-view" in a particular context, and are feasibly to be realized.

Dewey wants to make more aware, more conscious, more deliberate, more responsible, what (as Holmes points out) judges are doing anyway, however much lawyers and judges may be averse to admitting it.

9

Karl N. Llewellyn (1893–1962): Legal Realism

Karl Llewellyn emerged from the Yale School of Law with highest honors and, after a brief stint in Shearman and Sterling, a Wall Street office, taught with distinction at the Columbia Law School and later at the University of Chicago Law School. Held in high esteem by his colleagues, but little known outside the legal profession, he was a man of many talents. He was a close student of the works of Max Weber, and he tried to keep up with the social sciences. He collaborated with the anthropologist, Hoebel, on a study of law among the Cheyenne Indians. His introduction to law study, *The Bramble Bush,* has become a standby. His massive study *The Common Law Tradition: Deciding Appellate Cases* is the most comprehensive analysis of how judges decide and should decide cases on review. His many articles, including the militant proposals of Legal Realism, have been published posthumously under the title *Jurisprudence.* Besides his inspiring and innovative work in the field of jurisprudence, Llewellyn was an acknowledged authority in the nitty-gritty of sales and commercial law. He also authored a volume of poems. He had a uniquely coruscating style; he never descended to the dullness of sheer acadamese or legalese. It was in his seminar at Columbia that I first became enthralled with the fascination of jurisprudence. It was there, I started my book on Judge Cardozo, who was inspired by Llewellyn and called himself a neo-realist.

In propagating the "movement" of Legal Realism, Llewellyn did not claim a high degree of individual originality. He conceived himself to be integrating and furthering the new empirical modes of approach which he detected in many advanced law professors who were fed up with the old "*formal*ism" and "*concept*ualism."

By that time the law in America had become a highly skilled and systematic profession. Law professors were charged not only to train lawyers, but to illuminate and improve the law and law study. The Legal Realist movement transformed the teaching of law and the practices of judges and lawyers.

Legal Realism

The term *realism* means so many different things in literature, art, and metaphysics that we should make clear at the start that Llewellyn was using the term in its most ordinary, commonsensible meaning. He wanted to be realistic in the sense of looking the facts in the face—what was actually going on—instead of regurgitating worn formulas which failed to reflect our actual current experience with legal institutions. He might have called it legal "empiricism," but that was a word which only philosophers use for what is experienced and observed. He might have called it legal "scepticism," but that term might have had a negative connotation, and Llewellyn's motive was to rebuild more soundly on the solid foundation of actual experience with the law. He might have called it legal "pragmatism," but it was hard to encapsulate the parallel philosophic "movement" of pragmatism; besides, pragmatism was a philosophic reference, and Llewellyn wanted to avoid philosophy. He might have called it legal "functionalism," but that term needed more explanation than "realism."

I think Llewellyn was influenced by the realistic literature in America following World War I, which abandoned Romantic clichés and went in vigorously for extreme realism in describing everyday experiences without idealization, depicting characters as products of social factors in the environment. The realism of Theodore Dreiser and Sherwood Anderson was intensified by James T. Farrell. One day Llewellyn said to me that I ought to read Farrell's *Studs Lonigan*, a novel about Chicago streets kids. I wonder if he knew Farrell was an admirer, even a disciple, of Dewey.

Llewellyn's Legal Realism carried such realism beyond Holmes's limitation. Holmes bid us look at what *courts* do. Llewellyn wanted to look at what *all* legal officials do in society as complex as ours.

Though the Legal Realists were of a reformistic turn of mind, they were less interested in feuding with traditionalist critics than with getting on with their programs of inquiries. Though each Legal Realist had some special interest. Llewellyn enumerates nine points held in common:

1. Law keeps changing.
2. Society also keeps changing.
3. Law is not an end in itself, but a means to an end.
4. The *is* and the *ought* should be *temporarily* divorced, while we get on with our inquiries of what is actually going on.
5. The traditional legal rules should be distrusted insofar as they purport to be descriptions of what is actually going on.
6. Legal rules should not be regarded as the chief factors in judges' decisions.
7. Broad rules of law should be broken down into narrower categories.
8. Specific consequences should be tracked.
9. A sustained program of attack and inquiry should be carried out along these lines.

In sum, we should recognize that both law and society are in flux and that law is simply a means to our social objectives. We should embark on an intensive study of law as it presently functions before making judgments as to what should now be done. We should be sceptical about rules of law as descriptions of what courts are doing. We should be sceptical about these rules as the main constituents of appellate court decisions. We believe extant rules to be too sweeping. Law must be evaluated in terms of its consequences.

A strong effort should be made to disinfect the inquirer's mind of any ethical considerations (as to what the law ought to do) while he is investigating what is actually occurring in the area of law which he is studying. This separation of *is* from *ought,* description from prescription, is only temporary, since the motivation of the Legal Realist in the first place is his concern about the inadequacy of traditional formulations and his conviction that some improvement is necessary. Evaluation should be based on objective study of the facts.

With regard to the first three common premises—the flux of law and society and the need to see law as a social means—Llewellyn concedes nondistinctiveness for the movement.

Appellate Opinions

Llewellyn, himself, took for his speciality the work of appellate courts, as he strove to improve their techniques of decision and opinion writing. Since law teaching had largely revolved around the study of appellate judicial opinions, Llewellyn's focal interest was a natural one. The realistic improvements he sought would involve law teaching as well.

Legal opinions are written by the judge after his decision has been reached. They are intended to make his decision acceptable. The format of the judicial opinion is in terms of deductive logic. But the opinion does not give us an explanation of how the decision has been reached. The process of decision making is what engaged Llewellyn's attention.

Traditionally the law is regarded as a system of rules. Llewellyn does not turn his back on law-as-rules. What he objected to is lumping all rules together without any discrimination as to their relative significance. Some rules, for example, are very well entrenched; others are lessers rules for lesser policies.

Legal rules are too broad, Llewellyn thought. For example we have judicial decisions on contracts, but business contracts do not work out in the same way as domestic contracts. Legal Realists depart from the orthodox ambition of widest possible generalization.

Better Predictability

Llewellyn argues that the kind of certainty purportedly found in the law is largely illusory. Traditionally we have been led to believe in more certainty in predicting what a court will do than is afforded by the traditional rules. Actually, Llewellyn urges, we will get better control of the uncertainties and the unpredictables if we engage in inquiry along the following lines:

1. We should consider the role inevitably played by the personality of the judge.
2. We should focus more on the interaction of the traditional concepts and the facts of the particular case.
3. Studies should be made of "typical" fact situations and their outcomes.
4. Intensive work should be done on the cases of a particular state.
5. Substantive rules should be reanalyzed in the light of legal procedures. The law should be restated in terms not of legal rights, but of remedies (what can be done).
6. Human behavior and ideas should be scrutinized in specific areas of business practice and in general customs as illuminated in the social sciences of anthropology, psychology, economics, etc.
7. The effectiveness of the lawyer on the outcome of the case should not be ignored.

These seven lines of attack are directed by Llewellyn to matters within the sphere of professional and academic legal discussion. But Llewellyn throws his lines out further. He considers the effects of the doings of courts (and other legal agencies as well) upon the general public, upon laymen, upon those Jerome Frank liked to call John Q. Citizen. Thus Llewellyn proposes an agenda for even more expansive study. He is thinking in terms of inquiry, of agendas of study, of a program of investigation. He would include in its range the general public.

Important among such broader inquires are

1. What law means to persons "in the lower brackets"
2. Why there is so much uncertainty in the activity and effects of the appellate courts
3. An investigation into the trial courts and lower courts, administrative bodies, and legislatures

The traditional manipulation of precedents left a lot up in the air, obscured by the myth of legal certainty. Llewelyn thought there could be a more realistic and predictable procedure. He proposed a conscious search for "wise" decisions. In the traditional manipulation of precedents, no one can tell when the court will, and when it will not, seek the *wise* decision. If the perspective were readjusted more realistically, the outcome would not only be more certain but wiser, more just, less "legalistic."

Contrary to the ritualistic assumption of traditional precedent theory, leeway is available in interpreting the precedents one way or another and in choosing among them by facing up to the policy considerations. There is rarely a radical overturning of precedent in the common law. Growth has been achieved in the common law through the centuries while "standing on" the precedents. Llewelyn wants to clarify and improve the way this is done. He wants it to be done more honestly and less surreptitiously.

Judges have previously thought they could find certainty in the legal rules alone. But this is illusory. A closer approximation to realistic certainty is achieved by seeking for the wise and fair outcome within the possible limits afforded by precedent and statute. Llewelyn wants to work more sophisticatedly within the existing legal system.

Normative Considerations

Is there, in this Legal Realism program, a normative (ought) side? There is none as of the time Llewelyn launched it. Legal Realists, he thought, will be preoccupied with the time-consuming work of getting at the actual facts. So much has to be done; so much has been neglected. Llewelyn was not interested in pursuing the normative side at this early stage, despite his great interest in improving the law.

In his later writings, Llewelyn carried out in great detail a study of appellate opinions in order to discern a superior manner of appellate decision making and opinion rationale. In his later book, called *The Common Law Tradition: Appellate Decision Making,* he forsook his role as the crusading critic and became an appreciator of auspicious appellate work, which he found to be quite common in enlightened courts. These courts had already sought to come to terms with reorientation of the past precedents in a wise way, in an effort to render justice to the litigants in the instant case as well as to lay down a sound rule for future guidance.

10

Benjamin N. Cardozo (1870–1938): The Judicial Process

Cardozo has been hailed by Dean Pound as one of the greatest common law judges. His opinions as chief judge of the New York Court of Appeals were widely followed elsewhere, even in England. When Justice Holmes died, it has been said that the whole country rose to demand that Cardozo be the one to succeed him on the Supreme Court. President Herbert Hoover was reluctant to appoint another New Yorker, along with Charles Evans Hughes and Harlan Fiske Stone, and another Jew after Louis D. Brandeis, and a Democrat to boot. But the leading Republican senator from the Midwest, Senator William E. Borah, urged it, and Justice Stone, a member of Hoover's "basketball" cabinet and a former dean of the Columbia Law School, offered to resign to remove the objection to another New Yorker. Such acclaim is rare indeed. But it is not Cardozo's eminence as a judge that detains us here. Our job is to note his contribution to the issues we have here been discussing. When an admirer, Professor Harold Corbin of the Yale Law School, asked Cardozo to come to Yale to deliver a series of lectures on jurisprudence, Cardozo replied that he was not competent to do that, but he would come and talk simply and candidly about how he goes about deciding cases as an appellate judge. These lectures led to his little classic, *The Nature of the Judicial Process*. Cardozo modestly wrote me that it would "over-dignify" his writings to call them a philosophy of law.

Cardozo, like all the rest of us, greatly admired Holmes as the titan on the legal scene of that generation. But, after all, it does not help a judge to be told, as by Holmes, that law is a prediction of what a judge will do. Cardozo proposes to tell us what an appellate judge does. The reader can readily observe how the thinking at Columbia—both Dewey's and Llewellyn's—influenced Cardozo, who had been educated at Columbia at the college, in graduate school, and then at the Law School; who was a trustee of the university and a friend of its faculty, including the philosopher Irwin Edman, who dedicated his book *Four Ways of Philosophy* to Cardozo. Cardozo called himself a neo-realist, and it is apparent, given my prior interests, why I chose to do a paper on Cardozo in Llewellyn's seminar; the paper into my book *Cardozo and Frontiers of Legal Thinking,* in which I linked Cardozo's opinions and his theorizing about them to the currents of Legal Realism.

Cardozo starts by affirming that judge-made law must be recognized as one of the "existing realities of life." The judge's opinion is really a "brew." The judge mixes into the brew many elements: precedents, logical consistency, customs, morality. The brew results from the judge's choices. (Cardozo's view might be characterized as the "brew" theory.) Sometimes these choices are left inarticulated, even subconscious. But the conscious choices can be spelled out; they do not defy analysis altogether. When the overt reasons for the decisions are "nicely balanced," however, the judge's choice will then be finally determined by his general philosophy of life, his outlook on life. Professor Kent Greenawalt, who teaches philosophy of law at the Columbia Law School, has recently argued that it could well be the judge's religion.

Cardozo notes realistically that judges, like other men, have a philosophy of life even if they know nothing of philosophy or do not call it a philosophy. They quite often say they are getting along without philosophy. But nobody can escape the inherited and acquired beliefs and convictions to which all of us are exposed.

The judge turns to the standard sources: the precedents, which can be overriden by a statute, which can be overriden by the Constitution.

Neither the statute nor the Constitution nor the line of precedents can be said to be always clear. Interpretation inevitably comes into play. Ambiguities have to be resolved. Hardships may have to be mitigated. The judge may have to fill in gaps and become a "judicial legislator." He will try to arrive at the meaning of a statute by searching out the intent of the legislature which passed the statute. If the questions never occurred to the legislature, the judge must try to guess what the legislature would have intended.

When we come to interpretation of the Constitution, Cardozo says flatly that "free decision" on the part of the judge has become the dominant mode of decision.

If no statute governs and the judge is remitted to the common law precedents, he is facing the complex challenge to which Cardozo devotes most of this book.

The precedents afford a point of departure. His first step is to examine them. They are his first step, but they are not the sole tools at his disposal. They are not, as Cardozo puts it, the "ultimate sources of the law." But if the precedents are plain, the process of following precedent, known as "stare decisis," suffices. The challenge arises when the precedents are not clear, when there is no decisive precedent. That is quite often the situation when a case arrives at the highest court of appeals. Here it is that the judge resorts to his "brew."

Before he gets to the ingredients of the brew, Cardozo pauses to remind us that behind the precedents hover the "basic judicial conceptions" which emerge out of the institutions of our society. They are the products of our habits of life. They in turn may serve to modify our habits of life in a process of interaction. Cardozo does not spell out these basic conceptions. He calls them the "postulates of legal reasoning."

The judge's undertaking is to "fashion" the law for the parties in the case and also for those whose rights will be similarly affected. In our legal system stare decisis—standing on precedent—involves the implication that every decision contains the germ of a future directive.

Cardozo opens by stressing that the legal rules embodied in the precedents are continually subject to reformulation. He considers them to be working hypotheses, as in science.

The changes often occur so incrementally as to be almost imperceptible except as we look back after the lapse of some years. It can be likened to a child growing up as he changes from boyhood to adolescence to maturity.

Cardozo analyzes the cumulative precedents to elicit a generalization as the appropriate rule of law he is fashioning. He does not see himself as making a deduction from "pre-established truths of universal and inflexible validity."

Writing in the decade of the 1920s, Cardozo gives us an example the "spite fence" of a half century before. At that time, in the open spaces of the frontier, the law permitted a person to put up a fence on his own property, even though it was to annoy and injure his neighbor, and even though he had no other reason to put it up. As social and business relations became more complex, the law had to be changed. A rule appropriate for a simpler community no longer worked. Instead of a man being able to do anything he pleases in his business, even to injure another, the reformulation came to be: he can never do anything in his own affairs for the purpose of injuring another, but must show some good reason. It became necessary, in the social interest, to reformulate the rule of law.

The underlying principle derived from the precedents is known in the law as the *ratio decedendi*. In arriving at this basic principle, the judge must learn to pierce through all the incidental remarks (known as "obiter dicta") which abound in a judicial opinion. The law is not an exact discipline like geometry, and each judge has his own style, just like baseball pitchers winding up. In analyzing a lengthy and involved opinion, it is not always easy to winnow out the basic principle from the chaff of surrounding exposition.

But extracting the principle is only half the job. The second job remains: to set the principle on its way, whether to reaffirm it, modify it, or even overrule it. It is at this point that Cardozo makes his most distinctive and significant contribution. It is here that the "serious business" of the judge is challenged. The course which the principle takes, the extent to which it may have to be reformulated, depends for Cardozo on four guides. His exploration of these four guides constitutes the bulk of his approach. He speaks of these guides as "methods" of decision, but they are not really definite enough to be called "methods"; to speak of them as methods is to give them a more systematic status than he really intends. Besides, the labels he has chosen for these "methods" are misleading when one considers their context. These four guides are

1. *the method of philosophy:* along the line of logical connection
2. *the method of history:* along the line of historical development

3. *the method of tradition:* along the line of the customs of the community
4. *the method of sociology:* along the lines of justice, morals, social welfare, and the mores of the day

His "method of philosophy" is nothing else than the simple analogical process of showing the consistency between the precedents and the case up for decision.

We can designate these guides by alternative expressions which Cardozo sometimes employs:

1. the guide from analogy
2. the guide from history
3. the guide from custom
4. the guide from social values

The guide from analogy is put first because it is the "everyday" practice in our precedent system of law. There is a presumption in its favor if the other guides do not require that it be subordinated or sacrificed.

Cardozo waffles among the guides because no one can say with precision how to choose among them. "Much must be left to that deftness in the use of tools" which practice engenders.

We need the second guide, the guide from history, because some doctrines of law can be understood only as historical growths. In such cases history will predominate over logic or analogy. The best example is the law of real property. The law reflects the feudal tenures of medieval times as in the various types of "estates." These types of estates were never developed by logical deduction from any idea of ownership. On such subjects he quotes Holmes, "a page of history is worth a volume of logic."

If the first two guides do not fix the direction, the guide from custom may step in. Custom is credited with much creative energy in developing the common law. Lord Mansfield brought in the "law merchants," the customs of merchants at the fairs. In the law of sales today, recourse to the custom of a trade is made the standard in settling a dispute.

A slight extension of "custom" identifies it with "customary morality." Here we make the transition to the fourth guide, which

Cardozo calls the method of "sociology," and which I called the guide from "social values" because Cardozo embraces also the ideals of the society and not only its mores. Sometimes he speaks of it as a response to "social needs." Sometimes he speaks of it as the greatest force of them all in his generation: the power of "social justice."

In the last analysis, we are confronted with the ethical factors that can no more be excluded than can air from the room in which we breathe. "Logic and history and custom have their place. We will shape the law to conform to them when we may: but only within bounds. The end that the law serves will dominate them all."

Cardozo has difficulty in characterizing the "social welfare." He concedes that it is too vague and loose a term to satisfy a precisionistic philosopher. But he is satisfied that it is a term which "will at least be found sufficiently definite and inclusive to suit the purpose of the judge."

I quote a few lines to indicate the grab bag of ideas which Cardozo comprises under social welfare:

> It may mean what is commonly spoken of as public policy, the good of the collective body. In such cases its demands are often those of mere expediency or prudence. It may mean on the other hand the social gain that is wrought by adherence to the standards of right conduct, which finds expression in the *mores* of the community. In such cases, its demands are those of religion or of ethics or of the social sense of justice, whether formulated in creed or system, or immanent in the common mind.

How does one find a single term, he asks, to cover "these and kindred aims which shade off into one another by imperceptible gradations"?

(Picture Cardozo saying all that before a Senate committee passing on his qualifications! Picture an "analytic" philosopher flying into a rage at the lack of logico-linguistic rigor!)

"Social welfare" may mean what lawyers call "public policy"; that is, what is good for our society. Thus it is against public policy to enforce a contract to do a criminal act.

Or "social welfare" may mean some standard higher than "mere expediency or prudence": a standard of "right conduct." Perhaps it could be called the demand of the "social sense of justice" or the demand of "ethics" or "religion."

However we express or encompass it, Cardozo does definitely wish to promote attention to the social value of a rule: "It is true, I think, in every department of the law that the social value of a rule has become a test of growing power and importance."

Here Cardozo is clearly following the lead of Pound and Llewellyn, of sociological jurisprudence and Legal Realism, in advancing from a mere analytical to a functional attitude, to a consideration of the law in action.

This test of the social value of a rule, he points out, is primary in Constitutional law, but it is also relevant in other branches of law, where it is not so insistent and pervasive, but filters down from the background and emerges to the front when undue claims are pressed by tradition or logic or technicalities.

Toward the end, he quotes with approval the cautionary summary of an English judge, Sir James Parker:

> Our common law system consists in applying to new combinations of circumstances those rules of law which we derive from legal principles and judicial precedents . . . and we are not at liberty to reject them and abandon all analogy to them . . . because we think the rules are not as convenient and reasonable as we ourselves could have devised.

11

Lon Fuller (1902–1978): The Rise of Law

Ensconced at Harvard Law School as professor of jurisprudence, Lon Fuller has had the courage and independence to put Holmes and Legal Realism into a perspective which also makes room for natural law theorizing. While he purports to respect both legal positivism and natural law and to encompass a role for both, he is also encouraging a renewed respect for natural law in a new and secular way. That his heart is with natural law theorists emerges in his debate with H. L. A. Hart, who defended legal positivism against Fuller's criticisms.

He early criticized Legal Realism in his book *Law in Quest of Itself*. He elaborated his views in *The Morality of Law* and *Anatomy of Law*. In the famous debate with H. L. A. Hart, the leading English legal positivist, he strongly defended his natural law approach. In the account which follows, I have summarized his imaginative portrayal of the rise of the judicial process.

How would "judging" function in some newly formed society? There are no precedents; there are not even any customs, nor, of course, any statutes. It is as though a group of shipwrecked men were in some isolated corner of the globe and had lost their memories. What would they do? Fuller assumes men would naturally know what to do and that they would naturally do what he describes them as doing.

Disputes are bound to arise.

There must be some means provided to settle them. Some one is designated to settle them. We may call him a judge. We assume that he is reasonably intelligent. He feels a sense of responsibility for the well-being of the group and its morality as he goes about the business of deciding the disputes.

His decisions would not be mere expressions of his personal predilection. He would surely know that his task involved certain limitations:

1. As a matter of human nature, he would know that his decisions would come to be looked upon as precedents, especially if there were recurring patterns for ordinary situations.
2. He would foresee that, out of his treatment of individual cases, a body of rules would emerge. The community, in some degree, would tend to adjust to these rules.
3. He would feel that his decisions should be considered right—in the light of the group's common purpose and efforts.

> Such a judge would find himself driven into an attempt to discover the natural principles underlying group life, so that his decisions might conform to them. He would properly feel that he, no less than the engineers and carpenters and cooks of the company, was faced with the task of mastering a segment of reality and of discovering and utilizing its regularities for the benefit of the group.

He would be bound to see that his task required some study and reflection. But he also realizes that no amount of study could ever answer all the questions he must solve.

It would be clear to him that certain acts would have to be punished if the group's morals were to be held together. But when it came to the question of the sentencing, it would not be possible to discover any law which would tell him what the sentence should be. He would have to decide for himself in each case of a sentence of imprisonment whether it should be for a day, a week, a month, or for several years. At this point the judge will, himself, have to create the order to which men in that society will be expected to conform.

Thus the judicial process would turn out to be a combination: in part the discovery of certain laws required for a group; in part the imposition or creation of an order for the group. The former we may call the discovery of reason; the latter the exercise of judicial fiat.

In the historical vacuum with which we began, there was already an antinomy of reason and fiat. In a going society, with history being made, this antinomy becomes compounded, because the fiat which has become established by the judge has itself become a reality of which he must take account. This complication permeates the legal system. There are already many sources of positive law from which a judge draws his decision.

Because of the reality of this established fiat, complicated by positive law, it is easy to forget the basic problem. We lose sight of the fact that the judicial process remains a process of discovering and of applying those principles which will best promote the collective ends sought by the group.

What is really happening here is that we now have two recognized sources of law: established precedent and prevailing morality. The judge may decide to give preference to the prevailing moral conceptions in a given case and depart from one of his precedents.

There are other sources of law besides precedent and prevailing morality; there are business customs and scholarly treatises. The judge chooses among them. He is trying to decide what rule is best. Here is the real problem. When we ask which rule is best, we are asking: "Which rule most closely respects the facts of men's social existence and tends most to promote an effective and satisfactory life in common?"

It is unfortunate, perhaps, but inevitable that men must live in a state of tension of this kind. All thinking involves a kind of brokerage between opposing extremes. Notions which may appear to be contradictory form indispensable complements for one another. It is the antinomy of reason and fiat. Various schools of philosophy on one side or the other have leaned to one or the other side and have often tried to deny that the other side existed.

Natural law extremists have tried to eliminate fiat by maintaining that the whole of law is the expression of reason, or at least that it can be.

Extreme positivists try to cut the fiat loose from reason, though in recent years some, like Llewellyn, have said this was provisional only and for methodological purposes. To convert the whole of law into fiat we must identify the maker of the fiat. Thus custom could never be "law," no matter how sensible or widespread or conducive to public well-being, until it had been "stamped" by some authority—whether the judge (as in Holmes) or the sovereign (as in Austin).

If we turn from definitions and deal with law in terms of its problems, we see that law "is compounded of reason and fiat, or order discovered and order imposed, and that to attempt to eliminate either of these aspects of the law is to denature and falsify it."

Let us take as an example the fundamental legal concept of "ownership." Let us view it from the aspect of reason and then from the aspect of fiat. We shall then see clearly that we are involved in a circle and that reason and fiat are complementary concepts.

If a person owns a piece of land, he is protected by the law against trespassers. When he sues a trespasser, it is said that his ownership is protected through this suit in trespass. His ownership gives rise to this suit in trespass.

Now if one asks what this "ownership" consist of, we may say that it consists of the right to sue trespassers.

He can sue because he is owner (reason); he is owner because he can sue (fiat).

From the reason side, ownership stands for all the reasons of policy which would justify a court to proceed against the trespasser.

When we view it from the fiat side, ownership stands for the power exerted under the existing rules of law.

"The concept of 'ownership', in other words, contains within itself the antinomy of reason and fiat that lies at the heart of the whole legal order."

When we speak of the policy reasons justifying the court in protecting private property, we are confronting the philosophy behind private property. This institution is also composed of reason and fiat: much of it is founded on reason and, like all our institutions, it also has some arbitrary characteristics. There is both reason and fiat.

Now let us approach the concept from the fiat side. That is the way Holmes approaches it. A legal right is simply a way of describing that a legal remedy is available: "a legal duty so called is nothing but a prediction that if a man does or omits certain things, he will be made to suffer in this or that way by judgment of the court; and so of a legal right." Ownership is merely a way of expressing a prediction that the court will act to the advantage of the owner. The purpose of this Holmesian theory is to cut the law loose from the ethical considerations which have shaped it; or, in other words, to separate the law from its underlying reasons.

What did Holmes mean to say? Surely he was not saying that to speak of a man having a right is exactly the same as to speak of him as having a remedy. The term *right* adds something. What does it add? The term *right* is a generalized statement of the circumstances under which the remedy is available. When we say that a man, as the owner of his plot of land, has a right to sue the trespasser, we are expressing a prediction that he, and others in a similar position, will be granted a remedy. But when are others in a similar position? Once again we are led back into the realm of reasons as they underlie the institution of private property. "Our prediction of judicial action turns out to be meaningless unless we examine the reasons upon which judicial action is predicated, because it is only in this way that we can predict the scope of the anticipated action."

It is the same with other legal concepts: tort, contract, etc. They do not have two distinct meanings. Rather they stand for a relationship that can be viewed from two sides.

> When we view it from the 'under' side, we are attempting to find compelling reasons for the things that are done by courts in cases where these words are used. When we view it from the 'upper' side, we are attempting to present the action of the court as a brute fact divorced from the reasons that gave rise to it. Neither of these attempts is, or can be, successful. In terms of a physical analogy, both are like trying to produce a magnet with only one pole.

The natural law school cannot supply a rule which is purely reason. Neither can the positive law school supply a rule which is purely fiat.

It is easy to refute the natural law school by demanding a rule—even one rule—that rests on reason alone. This test cannot be passed. Suppose it is urged, as such a rule, that "men should perform their agreements." There are various agreements which the law will not enforce (such as a gambling or slavery contract). Thus, though many judges, in enforcing contracts, may have believed they were respecting a human need broader than any particular system of law, this purported principle of natural law would really have to be qualified. If a society wishes to enjoy the efficiency of division of labor, and if there is no caste system or slavery, then some agreements will simply have to be enforced by law, since the moral or social pressures do not suffice.

Thus we see that, though there are some human needs that are relatively constant, the concrete expression of these needs is always conditioned by some particular social context. The natural law school is never able to attain or exemplify its ideal of a system of legal rules absolutely or categorically required or demanded by the order of nature—and applicable to every kind of society.

It is equally true that the positive law school cannot supply a rule which is pure fiat. Take Holmes's famous definition: "The prophecies of what the courts will do in fact, and nothing more pretentious, are what I mean by the law." This view has developed a strong following and has given rise to a whole "school" of jurisprudence (Legal Realism). Yet no one can state a rule of law which is merely a prediction of a court's action without any reference for its action. Judicial action cannot be predicted (or discussed) except in terms of the reasons which give rise to the judicial action.

The value of a prediction that a court will decide in a certain way depends upon the basis of the prediction (or opinion). Why do we place reliance upon such a prediction? Because it is accompanied by the reasons assigned for the prediction, that is, how courts decide this and other similar cases: a generality. Thus we are involved in the basis for the rule—its foundations—its moral justification. We cannot state law purely in terms of the power of the court without any reference to any ethical factors.

Every rule of law is seen to embody this antinomy of reason and fiat.

The attempt to convert the law into a fiat of the state rests upon the notion of a sovereign who commands, as with Hobbes and Austin and their successors in the school of legal positivism. But what is the sovereign? The sovereign is the authority accepted by the people as the law-giving power. What is the basis of such acceptance? It rests upon a natural social order recognizing that life in society is impossible without some authority to regulate men's relations with one another. "The sovereign determines what is law, but is itself determined by law."

An authoritative deciding power must be present. But such power must be "legitimated." If it lacks the support of some rational (moral) principle, it "eventually frightens into a frustrated impotence both those subject to it and those who try to exercise it."

Thus we run the gamut from remedies and rights to power and sovereignty.

It is in dealing with remedies and rights (the "efficacy" of law) that the natural law school encounters its greatest difficulty. In this area of the law, the point of impact, the "arbitrary element is too obvious to be successfully denied."

It is with the most general notion underlying the whole legal system, notably the theory of sovereignty, that the school of legal positivism encounters its greatest difficulty. If law is defined as being what the sovereign commands, it is impossible to duck the problem of explaining why this law-giving power should be attributed to one source and not to another. Even the most extreme contemporary legal positivist, Hans Kelsen, admits into his theory a basic norm, resting upon what may be called the minimal natural law of the social need for peace and order, without which one cannot conceive of a legal system at all.

* * *

In this analysis Fuller is serving as a conciliator of natural law and legal positivism. Perhaps the fact that, in his own legal career, he has often served as an arbitrator has helped him to see the role that compromises play and how decisions can often be reached without overmuch reliance on definitive rules. He seems to be rising above both of the great "schools" of law and to find scope for each. But in view of the dominance lately of the school of legal positivism and the great prestige it has derived from the eminence of Holmes and his pragmatic variant, Fuller is really reviving a respect for natural law assumptions. But he is basing it not on theological, moral, or religious absolutes, but on what he puts forth as simple necessities.

12

H. L. A. Hart (1907–):
The Validity of Law

For many years H. L. A. Hart served as professor of jurisprudence at Oxford University. Hart originally trained as a lawyer but turned to philosophy of law as his exclusive preoccupation. He has made a vital contribution to contemporary jurisprudence in his masterwork, *Concept of Law,* as well as in other significant books such as *Punishment and Responsibility* and *Law, Liberty, and Morality.* His influence in America has been so great that I do not hesitate to include him among American fruitions.

Like many legal philosophers in the past, Hart sets out to answer the question: What is law? He does so in the Oxford mode of analytic and linguistic philosophy. In addressing himself to a dissection of the concept of law, he finds its illumination in an analysis of the elements of a legal system.

When we inquire into the nature of law, Hart suggests that we are really asking three questions:

1. How is law related to orders backed by threats?
2. How are legal and moral obligations related?
3. To what extent is law a matter of rules?

It is evident from the question which he poses first that his starting point is the Austinian theory. Indeed a substantial portion of his book is devoted to an analysis of Austin and the way in which, following in Austin's footsteps, he diverges from Austin's own formulation.

In seeking to answer these three questions, Hart is dealing with three social phenomena: (1) coercion, (2) morality, and (3) law. He wants to show us how they are related. He is not content with previous expositions of legal positivism.

His first question about orders backed by threats leads us to consider law and coercion. His second question about moral and legal obligation leads us to consider law and morality. His third question, about the extent to which law is concerned with rules, leads into his major claim: that basic to the concept of law is the concept of rules.

A significant portion of Hart's analysis is consumed with his basic distinction between two types of rules that he calls primary rules and secondary rules.

The Primary Rules

What are the primary rules? They are the rules people usually have in mind when asked about a rule of law. They are the rules which impose duties upon us. They are the rules we are required to obey. The best example is found in the familiar field of criminal law. A primary rule in the criminal law is the rule, for example, which prohibits murder. The law of torts—of private wrongs—also furnishes primary rules when it imposes upon us the duty to drive carefully or suffer the consequences of a lawsuit.

The Secondary Rules

Secondary rules are quite different. Instead of imposing upon us mandatory duties which we must obey (whether we wish to or not), the secondary rules actually confer a power upon us to realize our desires by creating obligation on others. Here the best examples are in the law of wills or the law of contracts.

When we make a will, what have we done? We have exercised a power, which we have by law, to create a legal duty imposed upon the executor of our will to carry out our wishes after we are dead. By going through certain procedural formalities, we have been able to effectuate our desires and the law will back us up.

These secondary rules were not attended to by Austin, who thought jurisprudence could be confined to coercive orders alone.

The Union of Primary and Secondary Rules

Hart claims that the key to jurisprudence is in the union of primary rules and secondary rules. All of the ideas and operation of law require reference to either or both of these two types of rules. Their fusion constitutes the essence of law. Hart submits that he has furnished us with the long-sought answer to the search for the distinctive feature of law as a means of social control.

Hart's conception of secondary rules also serves the far-reaching purpose of explaining powers of a public nature.

Since these secondary rules confer powers, these powers need not be only private powers to make a will or a contract. They may confer powers on public officials.

Take the secondary rules which confer power upon a judge. Rules such as these lie behind the operation of a court of law.

The same is true of the rules which lie behind the exercises of legislative power in a county or city.

When these secondary rules confer these powers on public or official bodies they are, in the first example, the power to adjudicate disputes which arise under the law—judicial power—and, in the second example, the power to make law—the legislative power.

We have now outlined Hart's analysis of the central aspect of the concept of law. Let us now turn to Hart's analysis of the related concept of justice.

As Hart remarks, justice is a concept of appraisal. In the family of words, its closet linguistic relative is *fairness*.

What Hart is preliminarily concerned to stress is that we should not confuse *just* with *good*. He wants to denote the word *just* as meaning something more specific than the more general word *good*. Justice is only a part or segment of morality.

What part is it?

We use the word *just* specifically when we want to appraise, not anything at all, but only when we want to appraise law. We use the word *just* to praise law and we use the word *unjust* to denigrate law. (This is a point, by the way, which Rawls overlooks or disregards in his recent masterwork, *Theory of Justice*.)

What then is the specific character of justice?

Justice denotes proportion or balance, as when we speak of the scales of justice. The central idea is: treat like cases alike and treat different cases differently.

That is to say, the principle of justice recognizes that individual persons are entitled to occupy a position in relation to one another of equality or inequality.

In order to say whether the law is just or unjust, we need criteria to determine when cases are alike and when they are different.

The first criterion is a formal and stable one. An example would be that a judicial proceeding should be impartial. The second criterion, however, is not stable, but varies, because it is not formal and depends on differences in moral and political outlook. The second criterion brings in nonlegal factors. With respect to the second criterion, the law itself cannot say what similarities or differences are to be recognized.

To appreciate concretely the special character of justice as a specific kind of moral judgment, let us consider two cases. The first case is drawn from our ordinary experience. The second case relates to the law.

If we observe a man being cruel to his child, would we not be inclined to say that he is doing something bad or wrong or wicked? It would not seem natural to say he is being unjust. However, suppose he arbitrarily chose one of his children and gave him a more severe punishment than the other children, even though they had all done the same thing. We should say he was unjust.

Now let us undertake to criticize the law rather than some individual.

If the law provided that we are free to criticize our government, we say we have a good law. We would hardly speak of such a law as a just law. But suppose we have a law which says that everyone, without discrimination, may use the public parks. We would call such a law just.

It is quite evident that *good* is a broader term than *just*. We may speak of a just law as good, but not the other way around. And justice or fairness is obviously not coextensive with morality in general.

Hart sees justice as a relevant moral consideration in two types of situations, which Aristotle perceived as "distributive" justice, and "compensatory" or reparatory justice. Hart invokes the same distinction, which he puts as follows:

1. We are concerned with justice as a distributive matter—the

distribution of burdens and benefits among persons. What is characteristic of fairness is their share. We are not concerned with the conduct of a single individual.
2. We are concerned with justice as fair compensation or redress when there has been some injury perpetrated.

Thus justice is something to be respected (1) when benefits or burdens are distributed in the course of our lives, and (2) when our life has been disrupted and there must be redress.

It now should be clearer why the idea of justice involves what persons are entitled to, in respect to one another, by way of a relative position of equality or inequality. Justice either maintains or restored a balance or proportion.

The distinctive value or excellence of justice must be distinguished from other social values. For example, if there is a severe rash of kidnappings or drug pushing, the judge may decide in favor of the sense of general welfare by giving people a greater assurance of security through exceptionally severe sentences. In doing so, he is departing from the justice principle of treating like cases alike. Also, there may be some instances where no compensation is available because it is thought that the general welfare of society cannot abide overburdening its courts. There may also be the case where someone must make reparation, even though he is not at fault at all, as in workmen's compensation statutes or no-fault auto insurance. The accidental events which these address occur so often and so disastrously that it is thought better for society to place the burden on those engaging in the activity, who may take out insurance. Though this is sometimes termed "social justice," it certainly differs from the kind of justice we have been considering.

In the name of social welfare, we often provide benefits for some at the expense of others. Examples are free education or aid for the poor. But such benefits are bestowed at the cost of other possible benefits, such as medical services. A choice has to be made in the interest of what is held to be the public good. The relation to justice lies in the demand that such choice should be made only after the claims of all interests had been impartially considered.

Hart also accepts a quotient of minimal natural law. It is a tribute to the flexibility of contemporary legal positivism and to the perdurance of natural law theory that Hart should have made this rapprochement. Minimal natural law includes recognition of the following:

1. *Human vulnerability:* men are both prone and vulnerable to violence, and hence there is a prohibition of killing or engaging in physical injury.
2. *Approximate equality:* no man is so powerful that he is able to subdue others, and thus there must be mutual forbearance and compromise.
3. *Limited altruism:* while men are not devils, neither are they angels, and hence aggressions have to be controlled, since altruism is both limited and intermittent.
4. *Limited resources:* because food, shelter, and clothing are not abundant, we need some form of property as well as reliance on promises.
5. *Limited understanding and strength of will:* some men who are able to understand these needs are sometimes tempted to place their own interests first, and hence reason demands voluntary cooperation in a coercive system.

In the absence of the recognition and acceptance of these truisms about human nature, men would not yield the voluntary cooperation which they do yield and which makes it possible to join in coercing others.

These are all natural necessities which constitute the core of good sense in the minimal natural law which must be heeded. They constitute Hart's rejection of the pure postivist thesis that law may have any content.

A close reading of Hart's footnotes reveals that this empirical version of natural law is divorced from any particular philosophy of life as to how men should live (in contrast to Aquinas, where the end is the knowledge of God, or to Aristotle, where the end is contemplation). This view of natural law is one based solely on commonplaces concerning human nature which simply cannot be disregarded. Hart's footnotes disclose his great indebtedness to Hobbes. This kind of empirical natural law, as we may call it, is even noted by Hume, who wrote that human association could never take place unless we heeded the "laws of equity and justice." As Hart says, in a vivid phrase, society is not a suicide club. Men wish to continue in existence, and hence certain actions are required for survival or, as he put it, "are naturally good to do." Thus among our social arrangements are some "which may illuminatingly be ranked as natural laws discoverable by reason."

IV

SUMMARY OBSERVATIONS

13

The Realist Outcome

In the United States in the early twentieth century, Austin's legal positivism, with Holmes's pragmatic variant prevailed.

Roscoe Pound, dean of the Harvard Law School and a colleague of William James, was inspired by James's pragmatism with its attention to human wants. He thought of the law as optimally satisfying human interests so far as feasible. The law has to weigh our diverse human interests. He called the process of weighing them "social engineering." He was a lone law professor in responding to the inspiration of philosophy—the philosophy of James as well as the philosophy of certain Continental jurisprudents. Morris R. Cohen, a student of James and the only American philosopher interested in legal philosophy at that time, welcomed this breadth of Pound. His "sociological jurisprudence," as he called it, laid the groundwork for the more militant and inclusive Legal Realist movement in the same direction, which was given its name by its chief protagonist, Karl Llewellyn. It is arguable that he did not give Pound enough credit for his pioneering.

Llewellyn launched Legal Realism as a movement by sparking and consolidating a trend among advanced law professors toward looking at what is actually being done, rather than being beguiled by legal rules alone. Llewellyn did not regard legal rules as otiose, but he was following Dewey's inspiration to go beyond the rules to all the activities of the world of law, including all legal officials and not only, as Holmes had led the way, judges. He said: let's be realistic; let's be empirical; let's describe what is actually happening. Let's postpone the normatives temporarily.

Jerome Frank was allied with Llewellyn in the initial momentum. Unlike Llewellyn, he was a trial lawyer, and he supplemented Llewellyn's "rule scepticism" with his "fact scepticism," which derived from his courtroom experience (which he called "courtroom government"). It is in the trial itself that we encounter all the quagmires of getting at the facts of what has transpired.

The myth of legal certainty, which Llewellyn was exploding on the appellate level, Frank exploded on the trial level. Frank performed a simple realistic service by breaking up the "judicial process," as Cardozo called it, into the two levels: the trial process and the appellate process. Law schools had been training students to become lawyers largely by critically studying the opinions of judges in appellate courts, which examine the evolving law case by case. As a law professor, Llewellyn concentrated his own realistic critique on the appellate process. He criticized it in his early work and, in his later work, based on years of empirical study of the actual work of appellate judges in various states, he appraised the ways in which he found it works satisfactorily. In making such a study, he was taking his own advice.

In the domain of philosophy, Dewey characterized the whole previous tradition of philosophy as a quest for an illusory certainty. Holmes put it epigramatically: Certitude is no test of certainty. Frank called Holmes the fully "mature judge," praising him in the nomenclature of a psychiatrist. At that time Freud was at the peak of his influence and in his book *Law and the Modern Mind*, Frank invoked Freudian theory naively to liken the law to a "father figure" as a rock of authoritative certainty. Frank likened himself to the little boy who cried out: the emperor has no clothes on.

In his second book, *Courts on Trial*, Frank was more reserved. His most provocative suggestion was that juries should be abolished because a juror is supposed to have the training of a historian in weighing evidence to get at the facts and jurors do not even have at least the discipline of learning of judges. Frank's book *Law and the Modern Mind*, came out at the same time as my book *Cardozo and Frontiers of Legal Thinking*, and Frank sent me many letters urging me to follow some of his more extreme realist thinking. But later Frank himself moderated his excesses when he wrote his second book, *Courts on Trial*.

How should we now estimate Legal Realism?

It sought an empirical account in observed experience of what is going on in the world of law, describing the whole spectrum of legal officialdom. It changed legal education and judicial awareness by alerting lawyers to the factors which really enter into an appellate decision, though unavowed in the formalistic conventions of judicial opinion writing. It stimulated social science studies of the consequences of laws. It documented the contention of Holmes in the law and Dewey in philosophy that the quest for certainty is an illusion. Thurman Arnold, a brilliantly satirical Legal Realist, said after a while that Legal Realism had done its job and didn't need any more developmental attention. Professor Walter Gellhorn has remarked that we are all Realists today. Professor Robert S. Summer contends that Legal Realism brought an entirely new way of studying and understanding law: where previously we had natural law, historical jurisprudence, and legal positivism, we now have Legal Realism as a fourth way, a new way, of handling the problems of jurisprudence.

We can no more capture Legal Realism in a formula than we can encapsulate pragmatism as a philosophy. Both are movements more than they are systematic crystallizations. Each of them is open-ended with ripple effects.

Llewellyn foreswore philosophy in favor of a social science type of development, having himself made an anthropological study of American Indian law. At the Columbia Law School, Professor Walter Gellhorn further remarked that the law school proceeds without philosophy. Many law schools do not teach legal philosophy at all and even at university law schools such a course is regarded as simply a course in theory, not mandatory, and not integral to the bread-and-butter, nuts-and-bolts courses which train the would-be lawyer.

Lord Evershed, Master of the Rolls in Great Britain in 1960, tells us that at that time anyone in England wishing to reflect on the broad problems of the law's philosophy would turn to the writings of the great American judges and law teachers of recent times: men like Holmes and Cardozo, whose book *The Nature of the Judicial Process* must always remain a classic. Since then, H. L. A. Hart in England has written an impressive book, *Concept of Law,* writing as a legal positivist and philosophic analyst. One of the most prolific analytical jurisprudents, Professor Ronald Dworkin, holds posts both at Oxford University and New York University Law School. He is a commuting Anglo-American, as it were.

Anyone who wants to study legal theory in England or America has difficulty following the polemics in the law reviews and philosophic journals. I hope this book will serve as an aide. The most agonizing phase of composing it has been the realization of what I was leaving out at every step of the way in order to achieve my goal of simplification. As Somerset Maugham has observed: "It is a platitude that simplicity is the latest acquired of all attitudes." Not many of my colleagues in this field have lived long enough to aspire to simplicity.

In concluding these summary observations on the realist outcome I am pleased to call special attention to the work of a Columbia University comrade-in-arms, Felix Cohen, who was writing on philosophy and law in the early 1930s, which is the focal period of my own involvement and of this book. In a fine article written in 1937, he lucidly appraised the developments to that date, making an assessment of Legal Realism and sociological jurisprudence from what he preferred to call a functional perspective.

In the pluralistic spirit of pragmatism, which is appreciative of other views, he asked what can be said about the merits of functionalism without derogating other approaches. Writing in 1937, he sidestepped the battling articles which followed after Holmes's "Path of the Law" (1897), and he published in an English journal, *Modern Law Review,* an article with the title "Problems of a Functional Jurisprudence."

Felix Cohen had unrivalled qualifications as the son and colleague of his redoubtable father, the rationalist philosopher Morris R. Cohen, and as one who had already taken a Ph.D. in philosophy at Harvard before studying law and graduating in the top of his class at Columbia Law School. Out of his broad erudition, he reminds us that intellectual advances have always been marked by focussing attention on theretofore neglected facts or issues which at the time were deemed unimportant. The pivotal figure in reorienting modern thought, Galileo, initiated the queen of the sciences, modern physics, by asking such questions as "How fast does a falling body fall?" In the prevailing theological and teleological atmosphere, no philosopher would bother about such a "trivial" question. (The philosophers refused to look into Galileo's telescope.) In our own century, non-Euclidean mathematical logic put Euclid in perspective by challenging his "self-evident" axioms. We also have Dewey's experimental logic of inquiry. The point is that new theories put new questions. They make a constructive contribution by putting these new questions, even if their theories are later overturned. Marx's theory has been discredited, but we still ask questions about how an event is related to how things are produced and distributed, and not only how they are related to the "sovereign." As we have already witnessed, not every legal philosophy is addressing the same questions. Legal functionalism for its part asks questions like: How do legal rules *work?* What are the *consequences* of a legal rule? What social institutions lead some legal rules to be *more effective* than others? Are legal rules given *ritualistic lip service* by judges with little relation to the *actual grounds* of the decision? When we ask questions like these, we are asking questions which were not asked by the natural law school concerned with the moral purpose of justice, or by the historical school concerned with how law developed, or the analytical school concerned with the structure of law. The functionalist asks new questions. In summary, the functionalist asks: What is the *human* meaning of the law? This question is simply a *departure* from prior schools of jurisprudence; it is not a question which *preempts* other questions or *denigrates* other lines of inquiry. The historical, analytical, and moral lines of inquiry are all interrelated with the new functional line of law-in-action. They are all interdependent. The "functional" approach has no pretension to substitute for these other approaches, but wishes only to supplement or augment them by focussing attention and inquiry beyond the legal rules to the law-in-action—how the law works, what its human social consequences are. No functionalist can function without also availing himself of the tools of analytical jurisprudence and of the light thrown by historical succession. But in passing moral judgment on law, functionalists believe that one must first have an honest description of how it works, how a legal rule (which is a prescriptive formula) functions in its human-social consequences. Because one must be able to find one's way through all possible consequences, criteria of importance must be selectively invoked. Here the needed inquiry must be an inquiry into value theory, and a fine contribution in that direction has been made by Abraham Edel.

Cohen sees Legal Realism and sociological jurisprudence as concerned with two basic issues:

1. Since the judge is the last word on the law, Legal Realism and sociological jurisprudence consider law as a function of what it is that judges do.
2. Legal Realism and sociological jurisprudence also consider law as it affects human-social behavior generally.

Those approaching the study of legal philosophy from the standpoint of philosophy rather than law will recognize the functionalist disavowal of the view that law or anything else has a "nature" or an "essence" somehow apart from its working interrelation with other things. As the word *functional* connotes, the special emphasis is on how the law functions or operates in our society. The eye is on law as a method.

Functionalism is a method. It is a method which says that to understand something it must be observed in action—as it operates—as it works—as it functions. It is a method common to the American "instrumentalism" of Dewey and the English "legal positivism" of Ayer. It was exemplified in the 1930s by Boas in anthropology, Weber in sociology, Laski (with whom Holmes constantly corresponded) in political science.

Since neither Legal Realism nor sociological jurisprudence are clearly defined "schools" of thought, but were movements with indistinct boundaries, Cohen observes correctly that they are not in opposition, but that in part they overlap and in part complement each other. Both spring from a "functional" outlook which may be said to bring a scientific attitude of mind to bear on legal theory.

It has taken so long to uncover the social contents of legal rules and concepts because they have traditionally been thought to be self-explanatory. Here is the statute: read it! Here is the judicial opinion: read it! What more is there to say? All the answers are to be found in the law books in the law library!

Functional jurisprudence flows precisely from the refusal to take at face value the rules and concepts, the statutes and judicial decisions. Consider the case of the statute on the books. Its words may not at all resemble the way it is working *in practice*. It may be a dead letter law. It may have been (and probably was) interpreted variously by different courts. No matter how much one studies the words of the statute in the books, it is not possible in that way alone ever to get a realistic picture of how the statute actually functions in its working out.

The same is true of a judicial opinion, in which the judge sets forth the reasons for his decision. Realists suggest one must seriously consider, as an integral part of law, factors which never get mentioned: the judge's educational background or lack of it, the power of his mind, his political or economic, philosophical, or religious beliefs, of which he may not even be explicitly aware. Are we to close our eyes to such obviously realistic factors and pretend, as with the proverbial calumny of the ostrich, that they do not exist? Are we to pretend that our precedent theory operates like geometry instead of being, as it indubitably is, a course of contingent historical events reflected variously and changefully and provisionally in judicial decisions? Things are what they are. Why should we wish to be deceived? Cardozo confessed to "a mounting sense of wonder with all our centuries of common law development" that "one has attained maturity without getting oneself in trouble when one has been so uncertain all along."

For centuries the extent of uncertainty in the law has been obscured by the legal fiction that judges have nothing to do with *making* law, but that all they have to do is *declare* the law as it exists. As Laski wrote in 1926: "The fiction that judges do not legislate has long since been abandoned by all who care for a conscious and realistic jurisprudence."

The law is a conservative institution. The fact is, however, that the judge usually has a choice between competing "principles" of law. We saw that Justice Holmes in his article, "The Path of the Law," candidly confronted the issue unabashed. The reader will recall his challenging exposé:

> The language of judicial decision is mainly the language of logic. And the logical method and form flatter that longing for certainty and for repose which is in every human mind. But certainty generally is illusion, and repose is not the destiny of man.

He goes on: "Behind the logical form lies a judgment as to the relative worth and importance of competing legislative grounds."

This judgment is often unconscious and inarticulated and yet it is the "very root and nerve of the whole proceeding." Holmes took straight aim at the judiciary, charging that judges have not adequately recognized that inevitably they have to weigh one social advantage against others.

What is, then, the research required if we would fully understand the course of judicial decisions? Where else can we go but to the burgeoning social sciences: psychology, economics, political science, anthropology, sociology, etc.?

We now turn to Cohen's second point: law as a determinant of human behavior generally. How does the law affect our conduct?

Jurisprudence has had hardly anything to say about the effects of the law on human conduct. That is because of the conventional and mythical presumption that everyone is presumed to know the law! As a matter of actual, realistic fact, of course, we are wholly ignorant of the law, and we often inadvertently violate or disregard it. How much a law is *actually* obeyed is a subject for functionalist inquiry.

We need a program for research in legal education and social reform. For example, to what extent can social reform legislation succeed if the public is not really ready for it? Laws are not self-executing. When the public is not yet fully ready for a social reform law, we have needed an administrative agency to oversee its enforcement.

What is the appropriate scope for law? Philosophers love to argue about it theoretically but the functionalist wants to consider the relevant empirical evidence. For example, is a particular social control simply a result of the power of the state or does it reflect a progress in legal wisdom or in the moral qualities of the citizenry? What is the relation of a given governmental control to the scope of religion, the educational system, the family, the self-policing activities of a profession?

The program of functionalism has not advanced very far in these areas except to call more conscious attention to the need. But the law has been able to draw on some studies by social scientists of subjects related to law: automobile accidents, union organization, corporate practices, the psychology of witnesses.

When the functional approach results in descriptions of factual situations, it has accomplished what Llewellyn (and Dewey) projected: a cognizance of legal *activities* and the human *consequences* of a legal rule.

But unless we idolize the status quo, we are still left with the second half of the problem which Llewellyn said should be postponed temporarily: an intelligent value judgment. Cohen believes we have to turn back to Bentham for this normative or ethical task. We have to start with Bentham's basic contribution to legal critique: that the value of any legal rule depends on its human consequences. That is the starting point. No matter what criterion of value one adopts, the essential core of consequentialism remains.

Why should we attach value to anything based on its consequences? Functionalists hold that we cannot really distinguish between a legal rule and its consequences. What is the meaning of a legal rule? The legal rule is seen from the perspective of the functionalist to be not simply a "command," as in Austin, but the engendering of an action. The legal rule, in its human meaning, causes certain actions to take place. A person must refrain from doing *this,* or he must do *that.*

Bentham's point, that the value of law depends upon its consequences on human conduct, could not be followed through in any detail in Bentham's time because the social sciences had not yet developed. Nobody had ever made a social study of a law case or compiled any statistical or other data about the consequences of a law. All Bentham could rely on was common observation. But since then, a wealth of material has been scientifically collected and organized, with several studies specifically tracing the effects of law in our society.

If we ask for a standard of value by which to determine what consequences are important, Bentham himself takes hedonism to be the standard: that the only good is happiness or pleasure. Cohen himself adopts that hedonistic standard, but he is fully aware that reasonable persons can differ on the standard, or even about whether there is any single or ultimate standard.

Nowadays, we do not so much speak of legal philosophy, jurisprudence, or legal theory. We simply speak of legal criticism or critique. In legal criticism the functional method has its due part to play. It starts with Bentham and the Utilitarian revolt. Its further broadening is toward relevant knowledge in the social sciences like economics and sociology. Scientific methods have been so productive in studying physical phenomenon for three centuries that the social sciences have extended it to social phenomena.

Not everyone may care to function as a functionalist in legal criticism, but functional criticism does give us clues as to how law operates as we go beyond its doctrinal bounds to become more realistic.

I am pleased to wind up this summary of the emphases in the legal pragmatism of the 1930s with a lucid 1960 retrospective by Harry W. Jones at the Columbia Law School. His article "Law and Morality in the Perspective of Legal Realism" is notable for his irenic determination to make peace between natural law and Legal Realism.

When Legal Realism first broke on the scene, some Thomists unleashed furious attacks. But in the retrospective calm of the succeeding decades, Jones is not only able to observe bonds of kinship with Catholic law schools, but, in this erudite article, he is also able to cite both Protestant and Jewish theologians as taking the same stance for religion as Legal Realism does for law. Whereas Felix Cohen proceeds from the scientific orientation of modern thought, Jones is concerned to show links with religious philosophy.

He rightly stresses at the outset that American Legal Realism is not a systematic philosophy of law but, as I have shown here, a "way of looking at legal rules and legal processes." If one associates philosophy with "generalizations," then a fortiori Legal Realism is no legal philosophy beause, as Jones identifies its core, it is a "sceptical temper toward generalizations."

He cites Llewellyn's manifesto of 1931, which I summarized, as the point of departure: "distrust of traditional legal rules and concepts" *insofar* as these are taken to be a *description* of what courts or other law-folk are *actually doing*. There is scepticism toward the conventional notion that rules are *the* "heavily operative" factor in court decision. That is to say, legal rules do not reflect what is happening, and legal rules are not the major factor in judicial decision making.

Jones quotes the well-known epigram of Justice Holmes, whom he calls "the hero figure" of the realist clan: "General propositions do not decide concrete cases." Though I am trying to restrict myself to empirical reporting in this survey, I cannot resist the temptation to retort: "Of course not. Judges decide cases. And anyway, it is half truth made for purpose of corrective emphasis: concrete cases are not decided without general propositons either."

Jones also quotes Holmes's most famous epigram from his book *The Common Law*, which has been so overquoted that I never cited it: "The life of the law has not been logic, it has been experience." Again I allow myself an interruption, to remark that Holmes means that the life of the law has not been formal, syllogistic logic. He would not exclude Dewey's logic of inquiry. And besides, experience alone is meaningless unless it is reflective experience.

Looking back at the embattled natural law critics of the 1930s, Jones remarks that one would have thought they would sympathize with the Realist claim that there is more to judical decision making than applying the generalizations of positive law. Jones wants to show that there are "far closer affinities between legal realism and natural law theory than exist between conventional analytical jurisprudence and the natural law tradition." Jones is able to cite Thomas Aquinas to this point.

Neither natural law nor legal realism accepts mere formal analysis of positive law. Basically both are more concerned with "justice in human affairs" than "doctrinal consistency."

Jones avows that though he is himself outside Thomistic natural law, he shares its view that the "great task of legal philosophy" is "moral evaluation." For this comment from a Legal Realist, he cites for an authority the words in the conclusion of Holmes's article "The Path of the Law," which always puzzles readers. Jones takes Holmes to mean that legal pragmatism is contributing to the "role of moral ideas in the functioning of law in society" when Holmes ends up by speaking of a "hint of the universal law." Be that interpretation as it may, Holmes certainly did urge attention to the ends of law. Jones himself winds up by suggesting that the "moral dimension of law" is to be found neither in rules nor principles, nor their higher law appraisal, but in the "process of responsible decision."

Jones does not ally himself with any existential philosopher, but he does invoke parallels in the views of the existentialist theologian, Paul Tillich, from his book *Love, Power, and Justice*. Tillich observes that every decision based on the abstract formulation of justice—and nothing more—is unjust. We can only reach justice by accepting also the demand of the particular situation so as to be "effective for the concrete situation." He asserts he has too strong a sense of the uniqueness of the individual occasions and the uniqueness of the individual facing it "to trust in general rules."

To Tillich's theological analogy, Jones adds a similar one from the Jewish existentialist theologian, Martin Buber. (Some "pragmatists" say that their own position can likewise be called "existential," especially since the 1960s when existentialism was much in vogue.) In spite of the similarities of every living situation, each situation, says Buber, has a new face, like a newborn child, and demands one's responsible presence.

Jones concedes that, though most appellate court cases can be decided readily by "traditional common law proprieties," the hard cases that cannot be so routinely decided, perhaps as many as a third by a loose guess, are the cases which constitute what Cardozo called the "serious business" of the judge.

It is in the study of the process of deciding such cases that the "moral dimension" of the judicial process is revealed.

In such cases, the judge's own "moral convictions" will have to be taken seriously. In such cases, "the resources brought to bear must be more than those of reason alone"; "moral courage and integrity are as important as intelligence." It is no abandonment of the law's confidence in its rationality to insist that "intellect and character are factors of equal significance in legal decision making." He again quotes Buber: "No book of rules" can be looked up to discover what is to be done now, in this very hour. . . . I answer for my hour."

Jones would have been even more persuasive if he had given many examples from run-of-the-mill situations. But instead he holds up to us *Brown v. Board of Education,* abolishing "separate but equal" education, and asks us to consider "the inner struggle, the turmoil of soul, through which a judge must pass in deciding a case of this magnitude." No one can suppose that the judge is mechanically following a rule.

In all such leeway situations, as in so many of the highly controverted cases which reach an appellate court, the *is*-ness of the positive law allows for alternative decisions. At some final point, the choice of alternatives will be influenced by the judge's "ought to be." Though with different emphasis, Legal Realism casts its vote with natural law and against Austin on the *complete* analytical separateness of the law that *is* from the law that *ought to be*.

Jones would not side with Fuller in obscuring the distinction between fact and value, but he wants to bring out that the dynamics of the judicial process are such that the ethical values of the judge can become a source of law in any given case.

Here Jones brings in the other Protestant theologian honored in our time, Reinhold Niebuhr, with his insistence: "The relativity of all moral ideals cannot absolve us of the necessity and duty of choosing between relative values."

For the "serious business" of the judge in making choices, Legal Realism provides a moral theory as demanding as natural law "but more directly addressed to the points of strain." In the Realist perspective, responsibility for moral choice in decision making becomes a central element.

Legal Realism departs from legal positivism in making this pragmatic recognition that fact and value are brought together when the judge has to decide a hard case. Judges always bring them together in deciding hard cases. But they have done so inexplictly, and it is the merit of Legal Realism to bring out into the open this moral choice among competitive advantages.

Through these summary observations I have sought to make more vivid and concrete the "realist outcome" of Anglo-American law as it came to a head in the movement of Legal Realism in the 1920s and 1930s. I conclude with a bow to Llewellyn, whose gusto and courage swept so many of us into this vitalizing trend.

In 1930 Llewellyn carried on his campaign in an article entitled "A Realistic Jurisprudence—The Next Step," which appeared in the *Columbia Law Review* but which had been originally presented to the American Association of Political Science with the title "Modern Concepts of Law." Throughout, Llewellyn is concerned with law in its social interactions. He is simultaneously addressing both law-folk, political scientists, and all those engaged in studies in the burgeoning social sciences. He applauded the breezy efforts of his fellow Realist, Jerome Frank, to let the whole public know about the reorientation.

Llewellyn emphasized that the engine of the law does not have any boundaries around law, nor any values of its own.

He reiterates his basic message. If we want to get a clearer grasp of the problems of law, we must put increasing emphasis on observables in our experience with law, and decreased emphasis on words. We must shift to the interaction of official behavior and those affected by it. Rules of law—principles of law—legal concepts should be encompassed in their bearing on these areas of social interaction. The emphasis on "paper rules" will fade as rules-with-real-behavior receive the importance due them.

The formulas of judges should be scaled by their frequency of "behavior-correspondence." The behavior of other legal officials should also be watched.

As the circle widens and attenuates around the center—which is the empirical emphasis—he adds that attention should also be given to any views being expressed about what the law ought to accomplish in some particular area. Still "farther from the center lies legal and social philosophy." The law overlaps with "other social sciences," which are not staked out like real estate.

To a radical empiricist or pragmatist like Llewellyn (even though he disliked labels like these), whose eye was focussed on primary, observed experience and its human consequences in their social settings, the logomachy among jurisprudents or legal philosophers would seem secondary and derived. It is as though religious people were asked to get involved in the quarrels among theologians. Theologians may come to get seriously concerned about arguments for the existence of God, say, but how much does the average religious person know about Tillich or Buber or Aquinas?

Envoi

The similarity of popular uprisings throughout the entire world as we enter the 1990s makes it possible for us to consider, for the first time in history, the realistic potentiality of a global common law.

* * *

We have reached the realist outcome. Law is seen as an institutional method for achieving social ends. Exploration of these ends in the framework of our democratic commitments as a free republic remains a continuous challenge.

A Bibliographic Chat

An exhaustive list of references, often more impressive than useful, would be out of place in a book of this tenor and, in this era of library computers, gratuitous. Instead, I'm recommending some books which are particularly germane to my purpose. Let me first give a brief synopsis of the themes to which my suggestions pertain.

After my account of natural law theories, I moved into the English movement of legal positivism, followed by the pragmatic turn given it in America by Holmes, followed by Pound's sociological jurisprudence, leading into the realist outcome of the 1930s in Legal Realism. I was also personally drawn into the Legal Realist movement at that time. In keeping with what William James called "pragmatic openness of mind," I have included thereafter Lon Fuller, who leans to natural law, and H. L. A. Hart, who from England turned even American attention back to analysis of the nature of law as a concept.

It is not necessary to supply references for versions of natural law, whether that of Cicero, Aquinas, or Locke, as they are readily at hand in encyclopedias, anthologies, and textbooks.

The line I have traced from Bentham to Austin to Holmes, and the outcome in Legal Realism, has to do with law proper and not the more dramatic issues of Constitutional theory which the Bork hearings have publicized. I find Holmes exemplary in his Constitutional theory in that he espoused due restraint for the Supreme Court in handling ordinary economic issues but not for civil-liberty cases, which have no support other than the Court's inspired reading of the Bill of Rights, facing down the government in behalf of the individual or minority.

In keeping with the streamlining aim of this book, I'll give only one reference for each of the English Utilitarians and the American figures:

Bentham: *Introduction to the Principles of Morals and Legislation*
Austin: *The Province of Jurisprudence Determined*
Mill: "On Liberty"
Jefferson: "The Declaration of Independence"
Holmes: *The Common Law*
Pound: *An Introduction to the Philosophy of Law*
Dewey: *Human Nature and Conduct*
Llewellyn: *The Bramble Bush*
Cardozo: *Paradoxes of Legal Science*
Fuller: *The Law in Quest of Itself*
Hart: *The Concept of Law*

For those who would like to go beyond Llewellyn's own work, I can recommend William Twining's book *Karl Llewellyn and the Realist Movement*. Jerome Frank's collected essays are in *A Man's Reach* (Kristein, editor). For second generation Legal Realists, I can recommend Harry Jones, *The Efficacy of Law;* Felix Cohen, *The Legal Conscience* (Kramer, editor); and Edmund Cahn, *The Sense of Injustice*.

For those who enjoy traditional philosophic discussion; I can recommend Huntington Cairns, *Legal Philosophy from Plato to Hegel;* for a textbookish account: Edwin Patterson, *Jurisprudence;* and *Men and Ideas of the Law;* for a brief summary, Martin Golding's article in the *Encyclopedia of Philosophy*.

Robert Samuel Summers's *Instrumentalism and American Legal Theory* is a sympathetic account by a student of Fuller and Hart. Carl Joachin Friedrich's *Philosophy of Law in Historical Perspective* is a product of Continental scholarship.

Scholars in law or the social sciences will find these a rich harvest to augment my account. Nonspecialists may also wish to peruse my other books: *Cardozo and Frontiers of Legal Thinking,* which contains analyses of Cardozo's judicial opinions; *Our Constitution: Tool or Testament?* which is a pragmatic account of Constitutional law progressing through Marshall, Taney, Holmes, and Brandeis, and *Corporation Lawyer*, which traces the transition of law practice to the office lawyer of our day.

Those who are interested in the strictly philosophic developments will find my comments on Abraham Edel's a wholly pragmatic alternative to legal positivism in *Ethics, Science, and Democracy*, edited by Irving L. Horowitz and H. S. Thayer (1986). A philosophic background with excerpts from each of the philosophers and acute analyses with the latest thinking will be found in *Morality, Philosophy, and Practice: Historical and Contemporary Readings and Studies*, edited by Abraham Edel et al. (1988).

Index

Adler, Mortimer, xviii, xix
Anatomy of Law (Fuller), 101
Anderson, Sherwood, 88
Aristotle, 5, 6, 112, 114
Arnold, Thurman, 121
Austin, John, xiv, xxvi, 22, 31–36, 57, 104, 106, 119, 127; legal positivism, 7, 19; objection to natural law, 30; *The Province of Jurisprudence Determined*, 23, 30
Autobiography (Mill), 37
Ayer, A. J., xxv, 10–11

Bentham, Jeremy, xxiv, xxvi, 19, 21–22, 23–25, 26–27, 127; *Comment on the Commentaries*, 22; *A Fragment on Government*, 22; *Introduction to the Principles of Morals and Legislation*, 22; *The Limits of Jurisprudence Defined*, 22; utilitarian philosophy and, 23
Berlin, Isaiah, xvii, 39–40
Berman, Harold J., xxi
Bernstein, Richard, xi
Bill of Rights, 14, 40, 44, 47
Blackstone, Sir William, 23; *Commentaries on the Law of England*, 13, 19, 21–22
Bonham's case (Coke), 13
Boorstin, Daniel, xxi
Borah, William E., 93
Bork, Robert, 14, 15, 40; *The Tempting of America*, 40
Bramble Bush, The (Llewellyn), 87
Brandeis, Louis D., 14, 72, 93

Brinton, Crane, ix
Brown v. Board of Education, 14–15
Buber, Martin, 130
Bundy, McGeorge, xxi

Cardozo, Benjamin N., xxvii, 8, 82, 84, 87, 120, 125; description of role of the judge, 94–99, 130; methods of making decisions, 96–97; *The Nature of the Judicial Process*, 93
Cardozo and Frontiers of Legal Thinking (Levy), xx, 94, 120
Cheatham, Elliot, xx
Cicero, Marcus Tullius, 4–5, 13; *De Re Publica*, 4
Cohen, Felix S., xx, 122, 124, 126, 127, 128; *Titles in Jurisprudence and Legal Philosophy*, xx
Cohen, Morris Raphael, xix, xx, 119
Coke, Lord, 12–13, 61–62
Collected Legal Papers (Holmes), xxv–xxvi
Columbia Law Review: "A Realistic Jurisprudence—The Next Step" (Llewellyn), 131–132
Command theory. *See* Law
Commentaries on the Laws of England (Blackstone), 13, 19, 21–22
Comment on the Commentaries (Bentham), 22
Common Law, The (Holmes), 49, 129
Common Law Tradition: Appellate Decision Making, The (Llewellyn), 92

Common Law Tradition: Deciding Appellate Cases, The (Llewellyn), 87
Competition, 68
Concept of Law (Hart), 109
Constitution of United States, The, 95; individual rights and majority rule in, 12
Corbin, Harold, 93
Corporation Lawyer (Levy), xxi
Courts, appellate, 90
Courts on Trial (Frank), 120
Cromwell, William Nelson, xv–xvi

Declaration of Independence, 44–45; Bentham's criticism of, 24–25; John Locke's influence on, 12
Declaration of the Causes and Necessities for Taking Up Arms (Jefferson), 43
Democracy, 40, 46–47; education and, 40
d'Entrèves, A. F., 30
De Re Publica (Cicero), 4
Devlin, Lord: *The Enforcement of Morality*, 39
Dewey, John, xv, xix, xxiii, xxiv, xxvii, 85, 94, 119, 121, 126–127, 129; definition of law, 82; *Experience and Nature*, 82; influence on legal realist movement, 81; social activities, law and, 84–85
Doren, Mark Van, xviii
Dreiser, Theodore, 88
Dunham, Allison, xx–xxi
Dworkin, Ronald, 121–122

Economics: law and, 73
Edel, Abraham, 123
Edman, Irwin, xvi, xviii; *Four Ways of Philosophy*, 94
Education, 47
Enforcement of Morality, The (Devlin), 39
English law, xxiv, 21. *See also* Law
Equality, 46
Evershod, Lord, 11
Evil, 34–36
Experience and Nature (Dewey), 82
Extant law, 82–83

Farrell, James T., 88; *Studs Lonigan*, 88
Feinberg, Joel, 39
Four Ways of Philosophy (Edman), 94
Fragment on Government, A (Bentham), 22
Frank, Jerome, xxv, 82, 120; *Courts on Trial*, 120; *Law and the Modern Mind*, 120
Frankel, Charles, xxi
Frankfurter, Felix, xix, 14; *Memoirs*, 78
Franklin, Benjamin, 45
Freedom, 20; individual, 38, 59; "positive", 39–40
Freedom through Law (Hale), xix–xx
French Declaration of the Rights of Man and the Citizen: criticism of, 24–25
Freund, Paul, xxi
Friess, Horace, xvi, xviii
Fuller, Lon, xxi, xxvii, 101–102, 107; *Anatomy of Law*, 101; judicial process and, 101–103; *Law in Quest of Itself*, 101; *The Morality of Law*, 101

Gaius, 6
Galileo, 122
Gellhorn, Walter, xix, xxi, 121
Glorious Revolution of 1688, 11, 13
Government, 45–46
Greenawalt, Kent, 94
Grotius, 6
Guide: from analogy, 97; from custom, 97; from history, 97; from social values, 97–98
Gutmann, James, xvi

Hale, Robert Lee, xix–xx; *Freedom through Law*, xix–xx
Hamilton, Alexander, 43–44
Hand, Learned, 14
Hart, H. L. A., x, xxvii, 101, 110–111, 112–115; *Concept of Law*, 109; *Law, Liberty, and Morality*, 39, 109; *Punishment and Responsibility*, 109; theories on nature of law, 109–110
Harvard Law Review, 50

Hedonism, 23, 127
Henry VIII, King, 8
Herzog, Paul, xxi
History of American Philosophy, A (Schneider), xviii
Hobbes, Thomas, xxiv, 6, 9–11, 66, 106, 114
Holmes, Oliver Wendell, Jr., xvi–xvii, xxiv, 14, 23, 61–62, 65–68, 74–76, 81, 82, 85, 88–90, 93–94, 97, 104, 105, 106, 119, 121, 128–129; "bad man" approach to law and, 50, 56–58, 59–60; *Collected Legal Papers*, xxv–xxvi; *The Common Law*, 49, 129; constitutional law and, 40; contract law and, 63–65; development of law and, 67–73; legal positivism and, 47–48, 50–52; "The Path of the Law," xxvi–xxvii, 84, 125–126; prediction theory of law and, 54–55
Hooker, Richard, xxiv, 8–9, 11; *Law of Ecclesiastical Polity*, 8
Hoover, Herbert, 93
Horowitz, Irving Louis, xxii
Howe, Mark de Wolf, 52
Hughes, Charles Evans, 93
Hume, David, 20, 29–30, 114; *Treatise of Human Nature*, 29–30
Hutchins, Robert, 9

Individual: interests, 78–79
Introduction to the Philosophy of Law (Pound), 77–78
Introduction to the Principles of Morals and Legislation (Bentham), 22
Ius civile, 6
Ius gentium, 6

Jackson, Robert H., xxi
James, William, xi, xxiii, xxiv–xxv, 77, 119
James I, King, 12–13
Jefferson, Thomas, xxvi, 43–48; *Declaration of the Causes and Necessities for Taking Up Arms*, 43
Jones, Harry W., xxi; "Law and Morality in the Perspective of Legal Realism", 128–131
Judges, 35, 36; appellate, what they do, 94–99; competing principles and, 125–126; decision guides, 96–98; intent of legislature and, 95; made law, 94; moral convictions and, 130; precedent following and, 95. *See also* Judicial process; Law
Judicial decisions: understanding of, 125–126
Judicial process, 101–103. *See also* Judges
Jurisprudence, 22, 27, 111; cultural, xxii; positive law and, 31; role of, 74–75; sociological, xxvii, 77, 99, 119, 124. *See also* Law
Jurisprudence (Llewellyn), 87
Jurisprudence (Pound), 80
Justice, 129–130; defined, 111–113; social values and, 113

Kelsen, Hans, 107
Kennedy, John F., 43

Law: American, 49; Anglo-American common, 54; coercion and, 110; as command, 33–36; components of, 104; contract, 61–62, 63–65; criminal, 34; definition of, 21, 82; as determinant of human behavior, 126–127; development of, 67–73; enforcement, 27; English common, 12–13, 19; extant, 8–83; functionalists, 126–127; global, 132; judge-made, 94, 125; legal duty and, 60–61; liberty and, 25, 39; logic and, 67–68, 70; malice and, 62; morality and, 27, 39, 56–59, 61–62, 63–65, 66–67, 110; nature of, 109–110; path of, 65–67; positive, 31; positive morality and, 32; positive versus scientific, 32; principle of utility and, 26; proceeding from superior to inferior, 36; punishment and, 24, 27; reason and fiat and, 103–106; social activities and, 83; social contract and, 9–10, 111; social control and, 111; social engineering and, 77–78; social good and, 79–80; social problems and, xix; social sciences and, 27; society and, 84–85; sources of, 103;

140   Anglo-American Philosophy of Law

state of nature and, 9–10; study of, 52, 55, 56, 72, 74–75, 88; study of economics and, 73; underlying principles of, 56. *See also* English law; Jurisprudence; Laws; Legal positivism; Legal Realism; Natural law; Prediction theory of law
Law, Liberty, and Morality (Hart), 39, 109
"Law and Morality in the Perspective of Legal Realism" (Jones), 128–131
Law and the Modern Mind (Frank), 120
Law in Quest of Itself (Fuller), 101
Law of Ecclesiastical Polity (Hooker), 8
Laws: moral, 24; social interaction and, 132; theological, 31–32. *See also* Law
Legal criticism, 127–128
Legal functionalism. *See* Legal philosophy
Legal philosophy, ix, 121, 124; legal functionalism and, 123–125. *See also* Philosophy
Legal positivism, xxiv, xxvi, 7, 19, 50, 101, 106–107, 113–114, 119, 131; extremists, 103–104. *See also* Law
Legal positivists, 105, 106
Legal predictability, 90–92
Legal prediction theory, 106
Legal profession, 52–53; basis of, 53–54, 57
Legal Realism, xxiv, xxv, xxvii, 71, 87–90, 94, 99, 119, 128–132; American, 128; basic concerns of, 124; criticism of, 101; movement, 81; New Deal and, xxiii; nine common points of, 89; outcomes of, 120–122; "Prospective overruling" and, xxiii; realism defined and, 88; sociological jurisprudence and, 124–125. *See also* Law
Legal Reasoning and Legal Theory (MacCormick), x
Legal rules, 81–82; and activities, 83
Legal theory: aim of, 55; American development of, 22–23; "bad man" approach to, 56–58, 59–60; "bad man" attitude and, 50; forces on, xxiii. *See also* Law
Legislature, 35, 36; law and, 34–35
Leviathan (Hobbes), 10
Levy, Beryl Harold: *Cardozo and Frontiers of Legal Thinking*, xx, 94, 120; *Corporation Lawyer*, xxi; *Our Constitution*, xxi
Liberalism: Utilitarian philosophy and, 29
Liberty, 25, 39–40; individual, 37; "positive", 40
Limits of Jurisprudence Defined, The (Bentham), 22
Lincoln, Abraham, 22
Llewellyn, Karl N., xix, xx, xxiv, xxv, xxvii, 81, 82, 94, 103–104, 119, 126–127, 128; *The Bramble Bush*, 87; *The Common Law Tradition: Appellate Decision Making*, 92; *The Common Law Tradition: Deciding Appellate Cases*, 87; *Jurisprudence*, 87; legal predictability and, 90–92; legal realism, 88–90; "A Realistic Jurisprudence—The Next Step", 131–132
Locke, John, xvii, xxiv, 6, 8, 9, 11–12, 25, 39, 45; influence on Thomas Jefferson of, 44
Love, Power, and Justice (Tillich), 129–130

MacCormick, Neil, x; *Legal Reasoning and Legal Theory*, x
McKeon, Richard, xvi
McLeish, Archibald, xxi
Making of the Modern Mind, The (Randall), xviii
Malice, 62
Mansfield, Lord, 97
Marshall, John, 13, 22
Maugham, Somerset, 122
Memoirs (Frankfurter), 78
Mill, John Stuart, xxvi, 5, 19–20, 25, 39–40; *Autobiography*, 37; individual freedoms and, 37–38; "On Liberty", 37–38
Modern Law Review: "Problems of a Functional Jurisprudence" (Cohen), 122
Moral duties, 26

Index 141

Morality, 24; judges and, 130; law and, 39, 56–59, 61–62, 63–65, 66–67, 110; malice and, 62
Morality of Law, The (Fuller), 101
Mysterious Science of the Law, The (Boorstin), xxi

Natural law, xxiii–xxiv, xxvi, 6, 9, 71, 101, 105–106, 107, 113–114; conflict with legal positivism, 7; conversion to natural rights, 11; criticism of, 23–24, 30; critics, 129; defined, 3–5; extant laws, compliance of and, 7; extremists, 103; human nature and, 9; law of nature and, 21; main constituents of, 7–8; minimal, 114; versus positive law, 82–83. *See also* Law
Nature, 3–4; reason and, 4
Nature of the Judicial Process, The (Cardozo), xx, 93
Niebuhr, Reinhold, 131

Oliphant, Herman, xix
"On Liberty" (Mill), 37–38

Parker, Sir James, 99
"Path of the Law, The" (Holmes), xxvi–xxvii, 47–48, 49–52, 125–126
Peirce, Charles, xvi–xvii
Penal Code, Model: of American Law Institute, 38–39
Philosophers: analytical legal, xxv; British empirical, 6; English "analytical", xxv
Philosophic Radicals, 23
Philosophy, xi, xvi, 120; American, xvi; American, of pragmatism, 77; American legal, 119; American pragmatism, xxvi; Anglo-American, of law, ix, 71; empirical, xviii, 7; English legal, 8–13; of law courses, xix; of pragmatism and law, xxiii; of stoicism, 3, 4, 5–6; Thomas Jefferson and, 43–44; utilitarian, 23, 29. *See also* Legal philosophy
Philosophy, academic, xv
Plato, 10

Pluralism, xi
Positive law: versus natural law, 82–83
Pound, Roscoe, xviii, xxv, xxvii, 77–80, 119; *Introduction to the Philosophy of Law*, 77–78; *Jurisprudence*, 80
Pragmatism, xi, xv, xvi, xvii; American, xxv, 77, 119; legal, 128–132
Precedent: cumulative, 95–96; following, 95; law, 97; ratio decedendi, 96
Precedent theory of law, 125
Prediction theory of law, 50, 54–55, 64–65. *See also* Law
Province of Jurisprudence Determined, The (Austin), 23, 30
Public mind: law and, 69
Punishment: law and, 27. *See also* Evil
Punishment and Responsibility (Hart), 109

Randall, John, xviii; *The Making of the Modern Mind*, xviii
Ratio decedendi, 96
Readings in Jurisprudence and Legal Philosophy (Cohen), xx
"Realistic Jurisprudence—The Next Step, A" (Llewellyn), 131–132
Reason, 6, 20
Reconstruction in Philosophy (Dewey), xvii
Reconstruction of Philosophy (Dewey), xvii
Reflective thinking, xvii
Reflective Thinking ("Columbia Associates"), xvi
Roberts, Owen, 14
Roman Empire: justice and nature in, 6–7
Roman law: study of, 74
Roosevelt, Eleanor, 45
Ross, Alf, 32
Rostow, Eugene, xxi
Rules: primary, 110–111; secondary, 110–111

Sanction. *See* Evil
Schneider, Herbert, xvi, xviii, xix; *A History of American Philosophy*, xviii
Social: values and justice, 113

Social activities: law and, 83
Social contract, 11–12; law and, 9–10; theory, 24
Social controls: law and, 111
Social ends: laws and, 132
Social engineering, 119; law and, xxv, 77–78
Social interests: law and, 78–80, 97–98
Social Order and the Limits of Law (Jenkins), xxii
Social problems: law and, xix
Social reform: legislation, 126
Social sciences: law and, 27
Society, 78–79; free, 38; law and, 84–85
Sociological jurisprudence. *See* Jurisprudence
Stare decisis, 95
State of nature: law and, 9–10
Stoicism, 3, 4, 5–6
Stone, Harlan Fiske, 14, 93
Stone, I. F., xv
Studs Lonigan (Farrell), 88
Summer, Robert S., 121
Supreme Court, 25

Teleological metaphysics, 5, 6
Tempting of America, The (Bork), 40
Theory of Justice (Rawls), 111
Thomas Aquinas, Saint, 5–6, 8, 13, 33, 114
Tillich, Paul: *Love, Power, and Justice*, 129–130
Torts, 69
Treatise of Human Nature (Hume), 29–30

Utilitarian: philosophers, xxvi; philosophy and reformist liberalism, 29; revolt, xxiv, 127; school of philosophy, 23
Utilitarianism, 19, 23, 77

Warren, Earl, 14–15
Weber, Max, 87
Wechsler, Herbert, xix
Wolfenden Report, 38, 40

Zeno, 3–4